The Trade Weapon

Tables, Figure and Boxes

Tables

Table 1 The armoury of the major traders 9
Table 2 ASEAN's value-added exports incorporated into other countries' exports 71

Figure

Figure 1 Anti-dumping and the business cycle 88

Boxes

Box 1 The UK and the China threat: the perils of a semiconductor sanction 54
Box 2 Global dependence on critical Russian raw materials 62
Box 3 The Supply Chain Resilience Initiative: it's the domestic economy, stupid 80
Box 4 Trade Policy Review of China: a mixed bag 95
Box 5 Trade law and COVID-19-related export restrictions: plenty of wiggle room 125
Box 6 Freer trade does not mean deregulation: US and EU treatment of Google 145
Box 7 The thoughts of Chairman Xi at the Twentieth Congress and what might have been 160

Contents

Tables, Figure and Boxes	vi
Abbreviations	vii
Acknowledgements	x
Preface	xi
Introduction: Free Trade's Winners and Losers	1
1 Sanctioning Aggression	31
2 Arming the Global Value Chain	57
3 Trade Self-Defence	86
4 Battling for the Greater Good	113
5 Arms Control: Restraining the Use of the Trade Weapon	139
Notes	165
References	177
Index	192

Copyright © Ken Heydon 2024

The right of Ken Heydon to be identified as Author of this Work has been asserted in accordance with the UK Copyright, Designs and Patents Act 1988.

First published in 2024 by Polity Press

Polity Press
65 Bridge Street
Cambridge CB2 1UR, UK

Polity Press
111 River Street
Hoboken, NJ 07030, USA

All rights reserved. Except for the quotation of short passages for the purpose of criticism and review, no part of this publication may be reproduced, stored in a retrieval system or transmitted, in any form or by any means, electronic, mechanical, photocopying, recording or otherwise, without the prior permission of the publisher.

ISBN-13: 978-1-5095-5755-4
ISBN-13: 978-1-5095-5756-1 (pb)

A catalogue record for this book is available from the British Library.

Library of Congress Control Number: 2023934606

Typeset in 10.5 on 12.5pt Sabon
by Fakenham Prepress Solutions, Fakenham, Norfolk NR21 8NL
Printed and bound in Great Britain by CPI Group (UK) Ltd, Croydon

The publisher has used its best endeavours to ensure that the URLs for external websites referred to in this book are correct and active at the time of going to press. However, the publisher has no responsibility for the websites and can make no guarantee that a site will remain live or that the content is or will remain appropriate.

Every effort has been made to trace all copyright holders, but if any have been overlooked the publisher will be pleased to include any necessary credits in any subsequent reprint or edition.

For further information on Polity, visit our website:
politybooks.com

The Trade Weapon

How Weaponizing Trade Threatens Growth, Public Health and the Climate Transition

Ken Heydon

polity

Abbreviations

ACI	Anti-Coercion Instrument (EU)
APEC	Asia-Pacific Economic Cooperation
ASCM	Agreement on Subsidies and Countervailing Measures
ASEAN	Association of Southeast Asian Nations
BRICS	Brazil, Russia, India, China, South Africa
CAP	Common Agricultural Policy (EU)
CBAM	Carbon Border Adjustment Mechanism (EU)
CEPR	Centre for Economic Policy Research, London
CEPS	Centre for European Policy Studies, Brussels
CPTPP	Comprehensive and Progressive Trans-Pacific Partnership
CRISPR	clustered regularly interspaced short palindromic repeats
DPRK	Democratic Peoples' Republic of Korea
DSA	Digital Services Act (EU)
ECIPE	European Centre for International Political Economy, Brussels
ER	Enforcement Regulation for Trade Disputes (EU)
FDI	foreign direct investment
FSI	Foreign Subsidy Instrument (EU)
FSRU	floating storage and regasification unit
FTA	free trade agreement
G7	Canada, France, Germany, Italy, Japan, United Kingdom, United States
G20	group of twenty nations
GAO	Government Accountability Office (US)

GATS	General Agreement on Trade in Services
GATT	General Agreement on Tariffs and Trade
GMO	genetically modified organism
GVC	global value chain
ICT	information and communications technology
IEA	International Energy Agency
IMF	International Monetary Fund
INSEAD	Institut européen d'administration des affaires
IPEF	Indo-Pacific Economic Framework for Prosperity
IPR	intellectual property right
IRGC	Islamic Revolutionary Guards Corps (Iran)
ISEAS	Institute for Southeast Asian Studies, Singapore
ITC	International Trade Commission (US)
JCPOA	Joint Comprehensive Plan of Action (Iran)
LNG	liquefied natural gas
LPF	Level Playing Field (agreement) (EU–UK)
MC12	twelfth WTO Ministerial Conference
MFN	most favoured nation (treatment)
MIT	Massachusetts Institute of Technology
MPIA	Multiparty Interim Appeal Arbitration Arrangement
mRNA	messenger ribonucleic acid
NAFTA	North American Free Trade Agreement
NATO	North Atlantic Treaty Organisation
NBER	National Bureau of Economic Research (US)
NT	national treatment
NTM	non-tariff measure
OECD	Organisation for Economic Co-operation and Development
PTA	preferential trade agreement
QR	quantitative restriction
RCEP	Regional Comprehensive Economic Partnership
ROK	Republic of Korea
ROO	rules of origin
SCRI	Supply Chain Resilience Initiative
SOE	state-owned enterprise
SPS	sanitary and phytosanitary measures

SWIFT	Society for Worldwide Interbank Financial Telecommunications
TBT	Technical Barriers to Trade
TiVA	trade in value added
TRIPS	Trade Related Aspects of Intellectual Property Rights (Agreement)
TSMC	Taiwan Semiconductor Manufacturing Company
UNCTAD	United Nations Conference on Trade and Development
UNSCR	United Nations Security Council Resolution
USMCA	United States–Mexico–Canada Agreement
VPN	virtual private network
WHO	World Health Organization
WTO	World Trade Organization

Acknowledgements

Some of the ideas in this book have been a long time brewing. I would like to thank a number of people for helping them mature: Steve Woolcock and the graduate students on our course at the LSE; Patrick Messerlin and students at Sciences-Po; former colleagues at the OECD Sébastien Miroudot and Przemek Kowalski, whose thoughts on the supply chain were especially helpful; and Gary Banks for his insider observations on trade policy formulation and advocacy.

I thank particularly Peter Drysdale and Shiru Armstrong at the Australian National University for giving me the chance to write, and draw on, pieces for the *East Asia Forum*.

My heartfelt appreciation goes to Louise Knight and Inès Boxman at Polity for their insights and commitment in turning a manuscript into a book. Thanks too to two anonymous readers for their constructive suggestions on things I thought were clear, but which obviously weren't.

And, as always, I pass my very special thanks to Katharina, for making it possible.

Preface

The past decade has seen a marked increase in the weaponization of trade in the form of targeted government interference with imports and exports and widespread resort to state-funded subsidies – all applied unilaterally or invoked in the name of goals that go beyond trade. The evidence is there to see – the stockpile of G20 import restrictions has grown more than tenfold since 2009 and continues to grow. And the increased frequency and complexity of distortive subsidies is – according to a collective report by the IMF, World Bank, WTO and OECD – bringing significant discord to the trading system. By strengthening the headwind against globalization, this is truly a collective own goal.

What has made weaponization possible? The simple answer to this question is the availability of specific weaponry in the trade armoury and the willingness of people to see it used. Despite over eighty years of multilateral trade negotiations and the plethora of preferential trade agreements – now covering over half of world trade – there remains considerable scope to use both tariff and non-tariff measures as a weapon. And the fact that trade opening creates losers as well as winners means that there is little objection to using trade restrictions to pursue other goals, whether the protection of human rights or the strengthening of scientific capability; most Europeans, for example, now have a positive view of protectionism.

The increased pursuit of those other goals is the result of longstanding concerns about national sovereignty combining with intensified geopolitical rivalry between America and

China and heightened concerns about supply-chain vulnerability, now turbocharged by the disruptions from the COVID-19 pandemic, the war in Ukraine and the challenges of the climate transition. As a result, we are seeing the trade weapon invoked in four interrelated and mutually reinforcing campaigns:

- to sanction aggression – whether cross-border, as with Russia's invasion of Ukraine, or internal, as with China's treatment of its Uyghur minority – in the interests of peace and human rights;
- to arm the global value chain in pursuit of increased self-reliance, as sought recently by the leaders of two countries among the greatest beneficiaries of open markets, France's Emmanuel Macron and China's Xi Jinping;
- to execute trade remedies in the exercise of self-defence, as with Donald Trump's – and now Joe Biden's – steel and aluminium tariffs, imposed unilaterally and invoking – somewhat improbably – threats to national security; and
- to 'serve' science in the interests of the environment and public health, whether via damaging restrictions on trade in key solar energy components or on the vital inputs to COVID vaccine manufacture.

In making clearer what we mean – and don't mean – by the trade weapon, care will be taken in these pages to see this growing and stark problem in its true perspective. Not all restrictions on trade constitute weaponization: there has to be unilateral application or an ulterior motive that goes beyond trade; and the trade weapon will not always be wielded with the intention to harm, as it may be seen as essentially a defensive arm. Care will also be taken to address the complexities of this subject: though our narrative starts with sanctions against Russia, this is not a strictly linear story. And there is an important difference in how we view our four motivations, in that, for sanctions against aggression, it is a case of doing them better, while for the other motivations it is, rather, a question of pursuing a totally different course of action.

So, who are the main protagonists in the weaponization of trade? Just about everyone, though this is essentially a big power phenomenon. Use of the trade weapon, as we will see, is system-neutral and wielded in autocracies as well as democracies – witness Russia's retaliation against Ukraine war sanctions or China's massive subsidy support of its state-owned enterprises. But the principal concern here is with the threat to the multilateral trading order when its custodians, the liberal democracies, act against the system they themselves created. For we need more, not less, liberal internationalism.

Weaponizing trade – with the ever-present risks of retaliation and protectionist capture – is bad for the world economy, as it diminishes and distorts the benefits of international flows of goods and services. Those benefits come not only from the stimulus to innovation that occurs when a firm – particularly one close to the technological frontier – is able to export and so operate in a bigger and more competitive market but also, crucially, from the improvement in domestic productivity that import competition brings. American, French, German and Japanese car makers, for example, all benefit from both effects. Open economies – giving full rein to comparative advantage – are richer overall and more productive than closed economies.

It follows that use of the trade weapon – whether in the form of US penalty tariffs on steel and aluminium imports, China's restrictions on the import of COVID vaccines and treatment, or EU carbon border taxes – always brings self-harm to the user. But co-option of the trade weapon is not only bad for global growth and development, it is also either counterproductive or, at best, ineffective in the pursuit of other goals. Fortunately, in each of the four campaigns of trade weaponry, there is a better way.

In this book, we'll examine each of those better ways, one by one: the need for diplomatic carrots to accompany the sanctions stick if Vladimir Putin and Kim Jong-un were really going to change their ways; for resilience in supply chains via sound domestic policy, not increased self-reliance through ill-advised re-shoring and friend-shoring; for multilateral

WTO remedies to rule breaking, not power-based penalties in the name of national sovereignty; and for direct action on environment and public health goals, not the blunderbuss of trade restriction.

But to restrain the damaging subordination of trade policy to other ends, governments, as well as seeking alternatives to use of the trade weapon, must address the discontents of trade. This means doing better at helping losers from trade opening, adjusting to technological change and making the case for open markets, not least by showing how use of the trade weapon brings harm to the user as well as to the target. All this will be taken up in the concluding chapter.

First, though, to set the scene, we need to consider what metal the trade weapon is made of, how the discontents of free trade help make its use so common, and why, in fact, free trade can be a force for good and should be encouraged. Without that encouragement, we are putting at risk three decades of global growth and development and the ability to deal effectively with the next pandemic and the climate transition.

Introduction: Free Trade's Winners and Losers

The pursuit of self-reliance through weaponized trade – whether by blocked Huawei access to US technology or subsidy-fuelled re-shoring in chip production – while not spelling the end of globalization, is seriously weakening the gains from trade while imposing a hefty, and mounting, bill on taxpayers.

Use of the trade weapon, in the form of targeted government interference with imports and exports and widespread resort to state-funded subsidies, has increased markedly in the past decade. It has done so because entrenched concerns about national sovereignty have combined with heightened geostrategic rivalry, notably between America and China, and worries about supply-chain vulnerability, turbocharged by the disruptions of the COVID-19 pandemic, the war in Ukraine and the tensions of the climate transition. The focus of this book will be on the four linked motivations[1] – or the four campaigns – for using the trade weapon.

The imposition of trade sanctions against aggression across or within borders is the first campaign to be addressed. Sanctions are a key element in the vicious circle at the core of this book, because sanctions disruption fuels fear of supply-chain vulnerability and favours the pursuit of increased self-reliance and global de-linkage, the second campaign. That pursuit of greater self-reliance, in turn, weakens trade disciplines embodied in the World Trade Organization (WTO), fostering unilateral, power-based 'trade defence' measures in the name of national sovereignty and national security, the third campaign. And unilateralism in trade defence, in its turn, by further enfeebling the trading order, helps encourage the fourth campaign, the co-option of the trade weapon ostensibly to help, but in fact harming, other, science-related, arms of policy in the service of the environment and public health.

But this account needs some nuance. What do we mean exactly by 'the trade weapon'? Of particular importance, care is needed to see this growing problem in its true perspective, not to overreach. Not all restrictions on trade constitute weaponization. The bulk of trade restrictions imposed in accordance with the multilateral anti-dumping rules of the WTO would not constitute weaponization.

For trade to be considered weaponized, one of two conditions needs to apply. The first is that trade restrictions are imposed unilaterally as an exercise in power, outside the disciplines of the WTO. The fact is, however, that unilateral trade measures, particularly in America and Europe, are on the rise. A second condition for weaponization is that there is an ulterior motive invoked that goes beyond trade. But again, the fact is that, while there is less and less support for the principle of a liberal trading order, those restricting trade nevertheless still commonly, and increasingly, do so by seeking cover under the invocation of goals that go beyond trade (and that cannot be justified under WTO exceptions). This means that, in effect, a large and growing body of trade restrictions do in fact constitute weaponization and, crucially – by virtue of protectionist capture – an augmentation and consolidation of the distortions to international flows of goods and services.

In practice, many examples of trade weaponization described in this book meet both of our two criteria. The Trump (and now Biden) steel tariffs, the European Union's Carbon Border Adjustment Mechanism, and China's import restrictions on COVID vaccines and treatments are all, as we will see, effectively protectionist but are invoked, respectively, and however questionably, to promote national security, the climate transition and national sovereignty. And all three are implemented under the authority of national legislation, outside WTO disciplines.

The trade weapon will not always be wielded with the intent of harming others. It may be seen as an essentially defensive tool. Brexiteers were motivated not by a desire to harm the European Union but, rather, to secure other goals, such as defending and promoting the Anglosphere. Restrictions on trade in gene-edited products are designed not to harm others but, ostensibly, to protect public health. The effect, however, of using the trade weapon will be to harm others, even if that is not the intent. Moreover, as we shall see, all four motivations for using the trade weapon described here do in fact embody an intent to impose harm, whether on, respectively, perceived aggressors, geostrategic rivals, sovereignty-infringing rule-breakers or suspected environmental free-riders.

Care is also needed to address the complexities of this subject, not to oversimplify. Though our narrative here starts with sanctions against Russia for its invasion of Ukraine, this is not a strictly linear story. Rather, the four motivations for weaponizing trade fuel one another more randomly.[2] The weaponization of trade did not begin in February 2022. Historically, the sanctions weapon goes back, at least, to the ancient Greeks. And, in practical terms, there is an important difference between the four uses of the trade weapon described here. For the three uses other than sanctioning aggression there is a better way than weaponizing trade, an alternative. And that alternative should be used. For sanctioning aggression, however, it is rather a question of how to make sanctions more effective.

This differentiation among the four uses of the trade weapon is not being advanced as a moral question. Clearly, there is a moral argument in favour of sanctions against aggression – such as that of Russia against Ukraine. But a moral argument can also be advanced, with disputable degrees of plausibility, for the other uses of the trade weapon: that denying China access to tech products in the global value chain is justified by the systemic threat China presents to Western values; that unilateral, power-based trade defence measures are morally justified when others breach commonly agreed rules; and that it is morally correct to impose import restrictions on products of environmental free-riders that put at risk the climate transition.

The case here for treating the policy implications of sanctions against aggression differently from other uses of the trade weapon is the fact that it is simply unrealistic to expect countries to forgo the use of sanctions in situations where human rights are being systematically denied.

So, what is it that draws our different uses of the trade weapon together? What do they have in common? It is the fact that, in purely pragmatic terms, these are the four dominant cases of targeted government interference with imports and exports and widespread resort to state-funded subsidies applied unilaterally or invoked in the name of goals that go beyond trade, but which are bad for trade, bad for growth and ineffective in attaining these other goals.

Critically, the weaponization of trade has been made possible – and that is the main focus of this introduction – because the arms are there and because people are happy for them to be used. The arms of trade weaponry, as we'll see, retain their potency because, notwithstanding the work of multilateral trade negotiation under way since the mid-twentieth century, the disciplines of the WTO are still incomplete and open to abuse, and the provisions of the 355 preferential trade agreements that are now the main game in trade diplomacy are inherently discriminatory. And people are ready for the trade weapon to be used because the presence of losers from market opening fuels the criticism that liberal trade policy is the major source of economic and social disruption.

Going back to basics – as we will here – shows that that criticism – and the trade weaponization it facilitates – is unfounded, and costly. The sixteen steel-using jobs lost in America for every steel job saved by US penalty tariffs will testify to that.

The arms

It may well be argued that both tariffs and non-tariff measures – the arms of the trade weapon – have been significantly reduced by the series of multilateral trade liberalizing 'rounds' since the mid-twentieth century and by the plethora of preferential trade agreements that have been signed since the 1990s. While this is true, the trade weapon is still highly potent. And it has been made more so by the broadening of the notion of 'trade' and by the advent of the global value chain.

The incomplete and vulnerable disciplines of the WTO

The tariff

The tax on imported industrial goods imposed at the border, the tariff, has seen a pronounced reduction in the past seventy-five years, with the average rate falling from some 40 per cent to under 5 per cent. This was achieved under the auspices of the General Agreement on Tariffs and Trade (GATT), founded in 1947 in the aftermath of two world wars and a global depression and driven largely by America and the support of the US Congress for reciprocal trade liberalization.

The GATT 1947 embodied non-discrimination in international trade. This was codified through the most favoured nation (MFN) principle (Article I) and national treatment (NT) (Article III). The MFN provision required that any favourable treatment, such as a reduced tariff provided to another – most favoured – nation, had to be extended to all contracting parties. National treatment required that all products imported into a country be treated the same as similar nationally made products, while nevertheless leaving governments scope to regulate.

Tariff liberalization under the GATT was to be achieved through mutual concessions that ensured 'global' reciprocity – meaning an overall balance of benefits as opposed to the narrower idea of reciprocity between specific sectors. Multilateral rounds of negotiation offered a means of ensuring that 'concessions' in areas of 'defensive' interest could be traded off against reduced tariffs in areas of 'offensive' interest.

Of the ensuing negotiating rounds, three stand out: the Kennedy Round (1963–7), the Tokyo Round (1973–9) and the Uruguay Round (1986–9), which, together, brought the average tariff on industrial goods down to less than 5 per cent. So, one could be excused for asking 'well, what weapon?'

Part of the answer to that question lies in two features of the tariff regime which mean that the average tariff conceals situations where the tariff is more onerous. First is the fact that low average tariffs mask large differences across product sectors. Because of the presence of tariff peaks, applied to particularly sensitive products, some 10 per cent of international trade in textiles, apparel and motor vehicles is subject to a tariff of 15 per cent or more (UNCTAD 2016). Secondly, tariff-induced distortions to international trade persist because of the scope for tariff escalation, whereby higher tariffs are imposed on consumer (finished) products than on intermediates and raw materials, thus favouring processing industries closer to consumers.

Beyond these two effects, it is often said that a principal reason why tariffs retain their potency as a tool of the trade weapon lies in the difference between bound and applied tariffs. Undertakings to reduce tariffs via GATT negotiations have been made in respect of bound tariffs: the upper threshold that countries undertake not to exceed. Actual applied tariffs, however, are almost invariably lower than the bound rates, meaning that countries retain the possibility – or the threat – of raising tariffs up to the 'legal' limit. In fact, this is largely an emerging economy phenomenon. As we see in table 1, both India and Brazil have a pronounced gap between bound and applied tariff rates. But for middle-sized players such as Australia and Canada the gap is less pronounced. And for the trading majors, the United States, the European Union and Japan, and indeed for China, there is little or no gap. In fact, the principal reason why tariffs retain their potency as a trade weapon is the possibility – and practice – of countries to exceed their bound rates – sometimes 'illegally' but much more frequently by exercising their legal right, within the WTO, to use – as something of a misnomer – non-tariff measures.

But, first, the irregular use. A relatively recent and widely publicized example of this came in 2018 when the Trump administration – unilaterally invoking US domestic law – imposed tariffs on the import of steel and aluminium that were far above US bound rates. Much more widespread, however, and totally within WTO rules, is the practice of imposing penalty taxes (in effect tariffs) as a defence against injurious activities by trading partners. The imposition of such penalty taxes falls within the broad range of so-called non-tariff measures.

Non-tariff measures
The scope of non-tariff measures (NTMs) matches the rather open-ended nature of their descriptor, covering quantitative import restrictions (quotas); barriers to public procurement; subsidies (domestic and export); a group of measures (triggering penalty taxes) variously described as 'commercial instruments', 'trade defence instruments', 'trade remedies' or 'contingent protection' and including anti-dumping measures, anti-subsidy countervailing action and safeguard action; and a set of measures covering regulatory requirements in areas such as public health and environment protection.

It is commonly said that, notwithstanding the continued relevance of the tariff, non-tariff measures have gained in relative importance. So, for example, we see that, while the United States and the European Union have relatively low tariffs on the import of motor vehicles from one another (2 per cent and 8 per cent respectively) the tariff equivalent of their non-tariff restrictions on motor vehicles is much higher (between 19 per cent and 27 per cent, depending on the methodology used).[3] A similar discrepancy is evident in transatlantic trade in metals, chemicals and electrical machinery.

This, however, is something of a sterile debate, given the important role played by the tariff in the 'non-tariff' area of trade defence (explored in chapter 3). But what is noteworthy is the extensive range of non-tariff measures, giving rise to a risk of multiple use.

Countries wishing to use the trade weapon to restrict imports often use a range of arms to accomplish this objective. The plethora of NTMs makes this eminently achievable. For example, restrictive sanitary and phytosanitary (SPS) conditions, strict technical barriers to trade (TBT) rules, non-automatic licensing and complex rules of origin may all be applied to the same product. When one impediment is satisfied or negotiated away, another may arise to take its place, thus frustrating market entry. This situation is often referred to as the whack-a-mole problem.

The existence of multiple NTM arms for the same product also creates problems for economic analysis, trade negotiation and policy making. While it may be possible to assess the total market distortion resulting from a set of NTMs, it may not be possible to measure the relative distorting effects of different measures and thus to establish priority when negotiating trade deals or setting trade policy priorities.[4]

Of the various GATT rounds mentioned earlier, only the Uruguay Round made a serious attempt to discipline non-tariff measures by introducing a 'traffic light' system to deal with subsidies, classifying aid as banned (red), potentially trade distorting and subject to countervailing action (amber) and permitted (green).

The reform process is, however, far from complete. This is particularly the case for trade in agriculture, where a recent report by the IMF, OECD, World Bank and WTO notes that, despite the longstanding mandate to establish a 'fair and market oriented agricultural trading system' while considering such non-trade concerns as food security and the environment, agreement on most issues remains elusive (IMF et al. 2022).

International reform efforts have been singularly unsuccessful in reducing resort to countervailing measures, as evident from table 1. Even more striking, the use of anti-dumping measures has continued unabated. This is particularly pronounced in the case of the United States, which at the end of December 2020 had 406 active anti-dumping measures in effect, covering no fewer than 416 products.

As indicated earlier, not all trade restrictions constitute weaponization. However, many of them do. And the sheer scale of distortions to trade gives an idea of the potential for unilateral and opportunistic resort to trade weaponry.

Table 1: The armoury of the major traders

	Tariffs bound rate	Tariffs applied rate	Anti-dumping measures (products) 31 Dec 2020	Countervailing measures (products) 31 Dec 2020
Australia	9.7	2.4	68 (58)	11 (21)
Brazil	31.4	13.3	146 (115)	3 (18)
Canada	6.5	3.0	96 (105)	29 (97)
China	10.0	7.5	110 (71)	6 (17)
EU	4.9	5.1	105 (186)	18 (86)
India	50.8	15.0	219 (414)	11 (33)
Japan	4.6	4.4	1 (336)	—
Korea	17.0	13.6	40 (34)	—
USA	3.4	3.4	406 (416)	140 (473)

Source: WTO, ITC and UNCTAD (2021).
Notes: Tariffs represent the average tariff for all products. Products affected by anti-dumping and countervailing measures are at the HS 6 digit level.

As touched on earlier, trade remedies are a particularly strong potential tool of the trade weapon as they carry the threat of an offsetting import tax (against alleged dumping and subsidies) that breaks the GATT commitment to both tariff binding and non-discrimination. We will look at this in more detail in chapter 3.

At the present time, a staggering one-quarter of imports in the world must comply with requirements for licences, quotas or other quantity control measures, representing half the value of total global imports (WTO, ITC and UNCTAD 2021). The potential to use quantitative restrictions (QRs) is the ultimate trade weapon, as QRs, unlike the tariff, totally preclude trade. QRs apply equally to exports, where they are permitted by Article XI of GATT 1947. In fact, the GATT has considerable built-in flexibility in the form of various exceptions to the rules that, in effect, can serve to strengthen the arms of the trade weapon. As Stephen Woolcock has observed, the range of exceptions mean that, rather than a charter for free trade, the GATT is best described as a system of managed trade liberalization (Woolcock 2012).

The principal exceptions articles in GATT 1947 – which, not surprisingly, feature strongly in our discussion of the motivations for using the trade weapon – are as follows:

- Article VI provides for the application of anti-dumping duties on imports that cause or threaten injury to a national industry and are sold 'unfairly' or at a price less than its normal value. It also provides for countervailing duties to offset the effects of a trading partner's subsidies.
- Article XI provides for export prohibitions (crucial to the discussion of sanctions in chapter 1) or restrictions temporarily applied to prevent or relieve critical shortages of foodstuffs or other products essential to the exporting country.
- Article XII provides for import restrictions to safeguard the balance of payments.
- Article XIV permits a temporary exception to the principle of non-discrimination in the application of import restrictions.
- Article XVIII allows countries in the early stages of development to grant tariff protection required for the establishment of a particular industry and to apply quantitative restrictions for balance of payments purposes.
- Article XIX provides for safeguard measures, whether tariffs or quotas, when an unforeseen surge in imports causes or threatens serious injury.
- Article XX provides a general exemption from GATT rules for measures necessary to protect human, animal or plant life or health (particularly relevant to the discussion of environmental and public health goals in chapter 4).
- Article XXI permits a contracting party to take any action it considers necessary for the protection of its essential security interests (relevant to the discussion of self-defence in chapter 3).
- Article XXIV offers an exemption from MFN treatment for customs unions and free trade areas.

The General Agreement on Trade in Services (GATS) has a comparable set of exceptions and flexibilities, including, under Article XII, the allowance of trade restrictions in the event of serious balance of payments or external financial difficulties. In addition, the GATS has exceptions linked to the way services are delivered – permitting, for example, regulation of the temporary movement of natural persons – and to specific sectors – as with prudential regulation in financial services. Finally, the GATS, under Article V, provides for the liberalization of trade in services among selected parties.

But an important qualification is in order here. The GATT and GATS exceptions, which as applied within the framework of the WTO must respect the fundamental principles of non-discrimination, coherence and proportionality, do not in themselves constitute the weaponization of trade. Their existence, nevertheless, can provide a supposed legal basis, or pretext, for weaponization. As we will see, this is particularly the case with GATT articles VI, XI, XX and XXI. A case in point is the 'anti-dumping' action taken against Australian barley and wine by China in 2020, widely seen as being invoked – weaponized – as punishment for Australia's call for an independent inquiry into the origins of the COVID-19 virus.

The GATT and GATS (in, respectively articles XXIV and V) also provide for the conclusion of preferential trade agreements. That leads to our next question: Why has the proliferation of these arrangements not disarmed the trade weapon?

The second best agenda of the preferential trade agreements

There are now 355 preferential trade agreements (PTAs) in force throughout the world, accounting for over a half of global trade. Should not the accumulated benefits of such a wide range of trade liberalizing accords severely weaken the trade weapon? In fact, less than one might expect, for four principal reasons: incomplete coverage, complex rules of origin, regulatory confusion and trade diversion – each providing opportunities for the weaponization of trade.

Incomplete coverage
Particularly sensitive products or services are frequently excluded from the trade liberalizing measures within PTAs. Compared with multilateral liberalization, plurilateral PTAs offer parties the opportunity to focus on carefully selected partners with whom it is possible – by a process of mutual accommodation – to liberalize selectively, albeit over a wide range of issues. PTA parties are thus able to exclude from liberalization commitments sectors that are politically sensitive and usually highly protected, while at the same time avoiding MFN commitments and associated concerns about free-riding by third parties.

For example, the PTAs of trading entities with strong protection of the farm sector, such as the EU or Japan, commonly have more restrictive provisions on agricultural trade. The opportunity then exists to impose restrictions by invoking goals that go well beyond trade, such as the preservation of traditional cultural values.

Then there is the complex question of rules of origin.

Preferential rules of origin
Rules are needed within PTAs (unless they are customs unions with a common external tariff) to determine which suppliers should benefit from any preference granted by the PTA. In the absence of internationally agreed rules, differing approaches have evolved entailing significant trade costs and complexity (Heydon and Woolcock 2009).

A graphic example of how rules of origin in preferential trade agreements can be used as a trade weapon is provided by the negotiations in 2018 that transformed the North American Free Trade Agreement (NAFTA) into the United States–Mexico–Canada Agreement (USMCA). US concerns related to the rising share of Asian value added in US imports under NAFTA prompted calls to further strengthen NAFTA rules of origin (ROO). As a result – and as now embodied in the USMCA, NAFTA's successor – the required share of a motorcar's components made in North America rises from 62.5 per cent to 75 per cent (what might be seen as the pursuit of collective self-reliance within the global value chain, as discussed in chapter 2). And up to 40 per cent of final assembly must be undertaken by workers earning an average of at least $16 an hour – seven times the average manufacturing wage in Mexico![5]

The third reason why liberalizing PTAs is only partly effective in taming the trade weapon is the challenge they present to international regulatory harmonization.

Regulatory confusion and capture
Notwithstanding the scope for regulatory cooperation within individual PTAs, the collective effect of preferential agreements in general is, rather, to foster disparity in regulatory approaches and, at worst, the use of regulation as a trade weapon. This risk is most apparent in the application of the WTO Agreement of 1994 on sanitary and phytosanitary (SPS) measures.

The SPS Agreement grants rights to take action to protect health and food safety, but only when these are necessary and when the measures are supported by scientific evidence (Article 5.7). Precautionary measures are possible when the scientific evidence is not available, but only on a temporary basis until the parties can gather the requisite scientific evidence.

In recent years, however, public opinion, notably within Europe, has shifted against a purely science-based approach following the failures of science-based regulation in the outbreak of BSE (bovine spongiform encephalopathy or mad cow disease) and various other cases. This has led to pressure for the use of the precautionary principle in the application of SPS measures. The result is a discrepancy in the regulatory approaches of US and EU PTAs, with the former relatively more science-based and the latter relatively more aligned to the precautionary principle (Isaac 2006). The ever-present risk is that the precautionary principle is used to block trade that might otherwise occur. Restrictions on trade in genetically modified organisms is a vivid example of this. By evoking concerns about public health, this is effectively weaponization.

And the final aspect of the limits to PTA moderation of the trade weapon is their impact on third parties.

Trade creation and diversion
The theory of PTAs dates from Viner (1950), who established that, if partner country production displaces higher-cost domestic production, there is trade creation, which is welfare improving. If, however, partner country production displaces lower-cost imports from the rest of the world, there is trade diversion, which is welfare reducing.

Two developments since Viner's analysis was formulated have tended to increase the scale of gains that might be expected from PTAs and reduce the expectation of third-country damage: New Trade Theory, allowing for dynamic gains through intra-industry trade, and allowance for trade in services, where discrimination is lower than in goods trade (Miroudot and Shepherd 2012).

While this is true, it is still the case that the gains from preferential liberalization will be less than those from multilateral opening – because of trade diversion. For this reason, PTAs are generally regarded as being 'second best'. The gains from PTA liberalization also tend to be relatively modest: only 0.34 per cent of GDP for the EU–Japan PTA, for example.

Importantly, for our purposes here, because of the reality of trade diversion at the expense of third parties, the choice of whether to conclude a preferential trade agreement with a prospective partner remains a potent arm of trade weaponry. This was made abundantly clear, for example, in the 1980s when the United States – anticipating the 'friend-shoring', discussed in chapter 2 – offered to conclude a preferential trade agreement with Australia but not with neighbouring New Zealand because of that country's opposition to port visits by US nuclear-powered naval vessels.

At this point we must conclude that neither successive multilateral trade-negotiating rounds nor the proliferation of preferential trade agreements have succeeded in disarming the trade weapon. Moreover, these shortcomings will become even more apparent as the notion of 'trade' and the way it is conducted are steadily transformed by the advent of the global supply chain.

Introduction

The transformation of 'trade' and its conduct within the global value chain

The fragmentation of global production is not new. But the scale of fragmentation under the recent period of globalization, or, as Richard Baldwin calls it, the second unbundling (Baldwin 2006), is unprecedented; over half of global trade is now in intra-industry intermediate goods and services rather than in the exchange of finished products.

The geographic separation of various production stages, which started in the 1970s in the United States and Japan, became more attractive in the 1990s with the continuing decline in trade costs due to the information and communications technology (ICT) revolution, the conclusion of the GATT Uruguay Round, the signing of the General Agreement on Trade in Services and the wave of preferential trade agreements. In the process, trade has become much more than a simple exchange of goods and services across borders, as it evolved into a constant flow of investment, technologies, goods for processing and business services in what has become known as the global value chain (GVC).

The transformation of 'trade' and the way it is conducted is important for two reasons. First, it means that, as the notion of 'trade' has broadened to take in more elements, each of those elements becomes susceptible to interventionist pressures, thus potentially increasing the potency and range of the trade weapon. For example, and we will see in more detail in chapter 1, the broadening of the scope of trade means that sanctions applied against Russia for its invasion of Ukraine in February 2022, such as denial of access to the SWIFT interbank messaging system and the prohibition of transactions with Russia's central bank, can be properly regarded as *trade* measures, within the broad category of trade in financial services.

Second, the transformation of 'trade' means that, as intermediate products and services become a more important feature of international commerce, with products and services crossing multiple borders, the opportunities for restriction at the border necessarily increase accordingly. The opposite is of course sometimes argued: that, as countries become more dependent on imported intermediate inputs, this increases the incentive to avoid impediments and higher costs in the acquisition of those inputs. This more optimistic view is not, however, borne out by the facts, with the stockpile of G20 import restrictions growing more than tenfold since 2009.

The GVC notwithstanding, tariff escalation is still prevalent, and even restrictions on intermediate inputs are still common. As a case in point, both the United States and the European Union impose stiff safeguard tariffs – under cover of the energy transition – on the import of solar modules and cells, even though these products are key components of the value chain producing – highly subsidized – solar energy. The outcome in this and other cases will depend largely on the relative political influence of the domestic producers of the intermediate input and of the downstream users of the input.

When a threat is all that's needed

As a final observation on the choice of arms when using the trade weapon – and as a further indication of their potency – on occasion the protagonist may find that it is sufficient simply to *threaten* action, without actually imposing any targeted restrictions.

A pertinent example of this arises in aircraft manufacture and the rivalry between Boeing and Bombardier. In 2016, the Canadian manufacturer Bombardier received an order for seventy-five C-Series (single aisle, 108- to 160-seat) aircraft from the US carrier Delta. Fearful of the prospective competition in its domestic market, the US manufacturer Boeing then made allegations of subsidy and dumping practices by Bombardier along the C-Series supply chain and appealed for protection. In response, the US Department of Commerce made a preliminary, unilateral recommendation, in October 2017, for protective tariffs against C-Series imports amounting to 300 per cent.

In an attempt to circumvent the threatened penalty tariffs, Bombardier then offered a controlling interest in their activities to the European aerospace firm Airbus, together with an undertaking that the C-Series, while continuing to be assembled in Montreal, would also now be assembled at the Airbus plant in Alabama. Bombardier's defensive response worked when, in January 2018, the US International Trade Commission ruled that Boeing had not been injured by competition from the C-Series aircraft.

While it might be argued that the threatened trade weapon succeeded in bringing Airbus skills into this venture, the result was in fact to further entrench the Airbus–Boeing duopoly in aircraft manufacture, further limiting competition, while also reducing the efficiency of the C-Series production chain by duplicating final assembly in two distant locations. The threatened use of the trade weapon served the interests of Boeing – without ever needing to be implemented – but at an overall cost to economic efficiency.

However – notwithstanding the potency of the *threat* of trade weaponry – it is only too evident from discussion in the main body of this book that there is plenty of follow through. And that happens, principally, because of the discontents of trade.

The discontents: the gains from trade

Countries shoot themselves in the foot when using the trade weapon because, by restricting and distorting the international flow of goods and services, they deny themselves the benefits of trade. Those benefits can still usefully be explained using the nineteenth-century construct of comparative advantage devised by David Ricardo ([1817] 1973) – one of the most widely cited and least understood principles in economics. The theory – or as the Nobel laureate Paul Krugman puts it, Ricardo's difficult idea – holds that the gains from trade depend on comparative costs within one country and not, as the earlier classical economist Adam Smith had postulated, absolute costs between countries. A country will gain by exporting the product in which it has a comparative advantage and – and this is crucial – importing the product in which it has a comparative disadvantage.

The theory of comparative advantage, developed by David Ricardo, can be explained using a simple model.[6]

Production	US one man-week	UK one man-week
Wheat	6 bushels	2 bushels
Cloth	10 yards	6 yards

In the case shown above, while the United States has an absolute advantage, in production costs, over the UK in both wheat and cloth, it has a greater comparative advantage in the production of wheat and will thus gain by exporting wheat and importing cloth. This can be shown arithmetically. In the US, without trade, 10 yards of cloth will exchange for 6 bushels of wheat. In the UK, by the same token, 6 bushels of wheat will exchange for 18 yards of cloth. If the US can get more than 10 yards of cloth for 6 bushels of wheat by selling wheat to the UK, it will gain by exporting wheat in exchange for cloth. Correspondingly, if the UK can get any more than 3⅓ bushels of wheat for 10 yards of cloth, it will gain by exporting cloth in exchange for wheat in international trade.

It was John Stuart Mill, the third great classical economist (after Adam Smith and Ricardo) who later determined that the exact terms of trade in between the two cost ratios – in this case between wheat and cloth – depends on the strength of world supply and demand for the two commodities.

The highly stylized nature of Ricardo's insight has been subject to considerable refinement over the years. In particular, the New Trade Theory of Norman–Dixit–Helpman–Krugman recast the gains from comparative advantage in the framework of intra-industry trade, increasing returns to scale, network effects and monopolistic competition.[7] Nevertheless, the essence of Ricardo's construct remains intact and relevant.

With the pronounced surge in inflation during the course of 2022, we have been reminded recently of one of the particular – and most important – benefits of imports within an open economy: combating rising prices. With US inflation at the highest rate for decades, and with US President Joe

Biden saying his 'top priority is getting prices under control', it has been estimated that a 2 percentage point reduction in US import barriers could reduce inflation by around 1.3 percentage points, saving the average US household some $800 over the year (Hufbauer et al. 2022). This would be consistent with other work suggesting that the relatively lower prices embodied in US imports from China have caused the US manufacturing price index to be 8 per cent lower than it would otherwise have been (WTO 2017).

The price change from tariff reduction would of course be a one-off event, while inflationary pressures result from an underlying excess of demand over supply. Nevertheless, the price effect of the lower tariff could, critically, help reduce inflationary expectations, which, once embedded in wages and prices, can push headline inflation even higher. The Bank for International Settlements, the bankers' central bank, spoke in its 2022 annual report of the danger of an 'inflationary psychology' that can spread and become entrenched. Recent studies suggest that, while professional forecasters and financial markets have expectations close to the Fed's target, consumers and firms have much higher inflationary expectations (Candia et al. 2022).

But, beyond this rather specific and immediate consideration, there is robust evidence that open economies are richer overall and more productive than closed economies. In concrete terms, it has been estimated that an increase in the share of trade in GDP of 1 percentage point is associated with an increase in income of some 1 to 3 per cent (Nordås et al. 2006).

There is here, though, a question of causality. The respected economist Dani Rodrik has suggested that, in the causal relationship between trade opening and economic growth, it is growth, via government support, that comes first and not market opening and outward orientation. In the ensuing debate, particular attention has been paid to the experience of Taiwan, which, along with Korea, was the first of Asia's 'miracle' economies. In their focus on Taiwan, Arvind Panagariya, Gustav Ranis and Ian Little have all offered a persuasive rebuttal of the growth-first argument.[8]

Taiwan's switch to outward orientation was centred on reforms over the period 1958 to 1960, when quantitative restrictions on imports were removed, quota allocations were streamlined in favour of exporters, the currency was devalued, export controls were removed, and inward foreign direct investment was opened up. Panagariya points out, importantly, that the currency devaluation would not have worked without the prior freeing up of imports (and thus of imported inputs to manufacturing) as it would simply have increased the price of imported inputs in the domestic currency. Critical to the causality argument is the fact that Taiwan's manufacturing exports – the target of the reforms – surged *in the wake of reform* and that this surge was *followed* by an acceleration in GDP growth.

The critique of Dani Rodrik (1995) has two elements: first, the timing of the market opening and the export response do not match – exports follow rather than lead the spurt in growth; and, second, when the growth spurt came, exports were too small to pull GDP ahead. On the first point, Rodrik rightly points out that Taiwan's outward-oriented reforms of 1958–60 were followed by a decline in overall exports. But this overlooks the fact that exports of manufactures – the target of the reforms – surged. The decline in overall exports was due to a sharp drop in agricultural exports; Taiwan specialized according to its comparative advantage.

Rodrik's second point, that exports were too small to pull up GDP at a faster pace, fails to account for the fact that a depreciation, such as that effected by Taiwan, increases investment not just in exports but in the entire exportable sector, including products that may not be exported at all in the initial equilibrium. As Bhagwati (1999) has argued, it is the scope for expansion at the margin rather than the initial level of exports that determines the ability of a sector to spur growth.

However, while we might accept that open markets bring an overall net gain to the economy, not all parties are affected equally. There are winners and losers. And it is this observation that leads to the most pervasive criticism of the liberal regime.

Winners and losers

Trade causes domestic and international prices, including wages, to converge, thus changing relative prices within economies and the returns to different factors of production – notably as between labour and capital. The most widely cited theoretical work building on this observation is the Heckscher–Ohlin–Stolper–Samuelson model. Elaborating on Ricardo's theory of comparative advantage, Eli Heckscher and Bertil Ohlin postulated that countries export products that use their abundant factor of production and import products that use their scarce factors. Building in turn on this work, Wolfgang Stolper and Paul Samuelson (1941) established that free trade increases the returns to the abundant factor *within an economy* and decreases the returns to the scarce factor. In practical terms, what this means is that trade will tend to favour skill- and capital-intensive activities in advanced economies and labour-intensive activities in developing countries. As with all theories, these propositions have not been without criticism; there has, for example, been some evidence of skilled labour making relative gains in developing countries.

Nevertheless, the broad lines of the theory hold firm as an indicator of the likely effects of trade and the expectation that unskilled workers in the advanced economies are likely to be among the losers from market opening. Hence one of the key reasons for the backlash against globalization.

In recent years, anti-globalization sentiment has been identified as a potent force on both sides of the Atlantic. In the United States, work by David Autor of the Massachusetts Institute of Technology and his colleagues found that American counties which were more exposed to imports from China became more likely to vote Republican in presidential elections – a shift which, it has been pointed out,[9] helped in 2016 to elect a trade-warring president (Autor et al. 2016b). In the EU, the Eurobarometer poll of July 2022 found that a positive view of protectionism is now the majority opinion in Europe. And, in Britain, Italo Colantone and Piero Stanig have found that concerns about globalization were an important factor in the Leave vote during the United Kingdom's Brexit debacle (Colantone and Stanig 2016).

Somewhat paradoxically, anti-globalization sentiment in the advanced economies, triggered largely by intensified competition from China, is matched by growing globalization scepticism in Beijing, where Xi Jinping's call for greater self-reliance reflects his belief that China has become too dependent on the liberal democracies. It is nevertheless within the liberal democracies that anti-globalization sentiment is most deeply rooted.

At first glance, the advanced economies' preoccupation with the negative disruptive forces of trade might seem well founded. There is now good evidence that competition from China in the 2000s has hit US employment harder than did competition from Japan in the 1980s, because Chinese products have impacted relatively more mature manufacturing activities that are less able to innovate (Eriksson et al. 2019). There is also evidence that the concentrated costs of trade opening can, and do, cause geographically concentrated job loss, with severe impact on local communities (Rajan 2019).

This said, it is necessary to set these negative impacts against the overall net gains that come from trade opening and the wider forces of structural change that are transforming developed country economies – within manufacturing and between manufacturing and service activities.

The decade leading up to the recession of 2008–9 is particularly instructive in demonstrating the positive role of trade. During this period, there was a sharp rise in trade relative to GDP, yet employment increased in all OECD countries apart from Japan, and the average unemployment rate fell from 7.2 per cent in 1995 to 5.6 per cent in 2007 (OECD 2009). In a complementary line of research, Robert Lawrence finds that the surge in imports from China in the early 2000s accounted for less than 5 per cent of all involuntary job losses in the United States (Lawrence 2017).

Some innovative recent work by Philippe Aghion, Céline Antonin and Simon Bunel helps explain the mixed character of the China shock (Aghion et al. 2021). Taking as an example the French automobile sector, they find that, if an import shock affects the (downstream) market for motor vehicles, then the auto firm's incentive to innovate decreases because the potential gain, or 'rent', from innovation is lower. Conversely, if the import shock affects the (upstream) market for auto parts, competition in the parts market will increase, production costs will fall, and the firm will have more incentive to innovate. Significantly, this work shows, empirically, that Chinese import shocks were more likely to occur on the upstream side of the production chain in France as compared with the United States.

But what of the charge that trade is a major source of growing *income inequality* in the advanced economies? Again, the case is not proven. Paul Krugman has thus concluded that some 10 per cent of wage inequality in the United States is attributable to trade (Krugman 2008). More recently, within a study for the French government, Dani Rodrik and Stefanie Stantcheva of Harvard University concluded that trade is but one of the sources of disruption in the labour market and far from the most important (Blanchard and Tirole 2021).

So, if trade is not the major cause of income inequality but, rather, it is domestic forces of structural change, what is it that has driven these forces? How can we explain the growing income gap in the advanced economies in the nineteenth century and the reduced gap in the twentieth century, up until the 1980s, after which the gap widened again?[10] Some recent, and ongoing, studies of this question have been undertaken by Thomas Piketty, Branco Milanovic, Jonathan Haskel and Stian Westlake. Their findings are not our prime concern here, but what is interesting to us is that none of their explanations attributes a leading role to international trade.

The explanation offered by Thomas Piketty (2014) is that there is a natural tendency, over time, for the returns to capital (including profits, dividends, interest and rents) to exceed the rate of growth of the economy, especially when the growth rate is low, leading inevitably to an increasing gap in incomes. He attributes the reduced income gap in much of the twentieth century to the effects of war, which saw both the physical destruction of capital and the necessity for increased taxation, narrowing the gap between rich and poor. This explanation, however, fails to explain why the reduction in inequality in fact occurred *before* the outbreak of the First World War.

An alternative explanation, offered by Branco Milanović (2016), is that the periods of growing inequality were triggered by Kuznets waves – named after the economist Simon Kuznets – of technological innovation that put a premium on skill- and capital-intensive activity, and hence on the returns to that activity. Kuznets suggests that inequalities increase in the early phases of industrial transformation because only a minority benefits from the new wealth that such transformation brings. The narrowing in inequality in much of the twentieth century can be attributed to progress in public education and a corresponding reduction in the skill premium.

A third proposition comes from the work of Jonathan Haskell and Stian Westlake (2017), within a growing body of literature on the prospects for economic growth. They argue that increasing inequality is linked to the fact that financial arrangements to support investment are geared to spending on capital goods rather than intangibles (such as research and development, marketing, design and branding) and that fostering investment in intangibles would encourage new ideas and create a larger pool of beneficiaries.

Whichever of these explanations is favoured[11] – and this is not our central concern – all three help to demonstrate that trade is not the principal motor of social disruption and income inequality.

Nevertheless, however persuasive the case that trade is not the prime cause of income inequality, winning that argument is greatly complicated by the role of interest groups and the risks of protectionist capture.

The role of interests and protectionist capture

Building on the distinction between winners and losers from trade liberalization, Vilfredo Pareto ([1906] 1971) postulated that the gains from trade opening tend to be delayed, dispersed and hard to measure, while the costs are typically immediate, concentrated and easy to measure. A case in point would be the closure of a garment manufacturing plant in the face of intensified import competition set against the price advantage eventually passed through to a potentially vast number of consumers. Put differently, by looking at the obverse of the coin: a protectionist measure provides large benefits to a small number of people and causes a very great number of consumers a slight loss.

It then follows, importantly, that political influence tends to be greater for those seeking government assistance or protection because those who stand to gain have more at stake than those who stand to lose. Relatively concentrated groups, whether geographically, by number of enterprises or by sub-sector (sugar producers have been major beneficiaries of the European Union's Common Agricultural Policy), are also better placed to meet the costs of collective action by monitoring political contributions or excluding free-riders.

These two elements of the political economy of international trade – the concentrated benefits of protection and the organizational strength of well-focused groups – help explain the enduring feature of protection: once protective policies are in place, they are very difficult to change.[12] Hence the unwillingness of trade negotiators, from both developed and developing countries, during the ill-fated Doha Round WTO negotiations that were supposed to complete the unfinished business of the Uruguay Round, to move away from the status quo.

Protectionist capture – though rarely acknowledged – is so pervasive that, as we shall see, it tends to permeate through all four campaigns of trade weaponry that we will be considering. Protectionist capture also knows no national or cultural boundaries, ranging over the power of incumbent educators in Egypt (Heydon and Makary 2006), the telecoms monopoly in India (Panagariya 2008), the four big incumbent retail banks in Australia (Productivity Commission 2018) and – perhaps most graphically – the big-farm beneficiaries of the EU Common Agricultural Policy.

Expenditure on the Common Agricultural Policy (CAP) as a share of the EU budget has fallen steadily, from 65.5 per cent in 1980 to 33.1 per cent in 2021. But it still represents the largest single outlay and, even allowing for the fact that farm support is the only EU policy funded almost entirely from the common budget, this is still a remarkably high allocation. Critically – and here is the key point in terms of protectionist capture – EU agricultural protection falls short in one of its most important stated goals: improving the livelihood of small farmers. Some 80 per cent of CAP payments still go to just 20 per cent of beneficiaries, and, in setting the CAP for 2023–7, the EU Agricultural Council refused to make the capping and degressivity of direct payments proposed by the EU Commission for large farms compulsory. It is this concentration of the benefits of protection that makes protectionist capture a defining characteristic of the Common Agricultural Policy.

But the interest groups affected by trade are not static; they evolve over time. As Douglas Irwin has pointed out, since the 1970s the focus of trade interests in the United States has shifted from industries to factors of production. As congressional attention has moved from tariffs to broad trade agreements, and with the advent of intra-industry trade (where industries are fragmented according to comparative advantage), economic interests are defined less sharply by industry and more by the intensity of factor use.

Within developed countries, the tension in trade policy thus tends to be between the interests (often import-competing) associated with the production of labour-intensive goods (likely to favour protection from imports) and those (often engaged in export) associated with skilled-labour and technology-intensive goods and services (likely to favour open markets) (Irwin 2017).

In recent years, resistance to trade reform has taken on a new and wider dimension as attempts at market opening have extended beyond the reduction of restrictions, essentially tariffs, at the border. With liberalization now tackling domestic regulatory impediments to trade in goods and, increasingly, services and associated investment, corresponding fears – notably in the advanced economies – have been triggered about perceived threats to the regulatory sovereignty of national governments. These concerns are being articulated by high-profile anti-globalization pressure groups and are particularly acute in respect of regulatory standards dealing with the environment, financial sector oversight, public health and public education.

The key point emerging here is that the backlash against globalization – and trade opening – is making it easier for targeted trade restriction and distortion – the trade weapon – to be used in the pursuit of the other goals that we will be considering, such as 'serving' science or 'promoting' peace – use that comes at a cost.

The trade weapon and the risk of self-harm

Among the most common uses of the trade weapon is the imposition of punitive tariffs on imports from the targeted country. The actual impact on the user of such a policy will depend on three related factors: the availability of substitutes, who pays the tax, and the effect on exchange rates.

In principle, consumers of a taxed import can seek alternative suppliers from countries not subject to the tariff. In practice, this may be difficult if the taxed product is part of an integrated supply chain. And, where a switch is possible, this will in any case mean turning to a dearer source (otherwise it would have been used in the first place).

The availability of substitutes may also bear on the incidence of the tax. Again, in principle, it is possible that a country facing increased tariffs in an important market, and in the presence of untaxed competing suppliers, will lower its selling price to maintain market share. In the case of the penalty tariffs on imports from China imposed by the United States in 2018, there is no clear evidence that this happened. This could have been because of the exchange rate effect.

Raising tariffs on a country's goods will reduce demand for those goods but also for the currency associated with them – effectively depreciating the foreign exporter's currency and appreciating that of the country imposing the tariff. In the four months following the imposition of US tariffs against Chinese imports in 2018, the yuan fell some 8 per cent against the dollar (prompting, somewhat perversely, accusations by the then US treasury secretary Steven Mnuchin of Chinese currency manipulation). The exchange rate effect may attenuate to some extent the negative effect of the tariff on imported inputs, but it will still mean reduced export competitiveness – via currency appreciation – for the tariff-imposing country.

In short, there is very limited scope to avoid the negative impact on domestic efficiency of increasing the tax on imports. Those negative impacts have been the subject of empirical testing by Jonathan Ostry and his colleagues at the International Monetary Fund (Ostry et al. 2019). The study, using data from 151 countries over a fifty-year timeframe, finds that tariff increases, as well as causing real exchange rate appreciation, lead to significant declines in domestic output and productivity, higher unemployment and higher inequality. The study also finds that the effects on output and productivity tend to be magnified when tariffs rise during economic expansions.

A particularly vivid illustration of the futility and cost of increasing tariffs is presented by the experience of the Trump administration in seeking to reduce the US trade deficit. In April 2018, President Donald Trump tweeted 'We have a Trade Deficit of $500bn per year. We cannot let this continue!' In response (and for other motivations), US tariffs, which in 2016, the year before Trump became president, were levied on just 2 per cent of US imported goods at an average rate of 1.7 per cent, by 2020 were being levied on 15 per cent of imports at an average rate of 13.8 per cent. However, over the four years of the Trump presidency the US trade deficit soared to its highest level since 2008, increasing from $481 billion to $679 billion.

Four principal factors help explain this exercise of self-harm: retaliation by the countries facing increased tariffs on their exports, notably China and the European Union; the switching of US imports from China to other sources; the contribution of the US tariffs to the appreciation of the US dollar; and the fiscal expansion undertaken during the Trump administration, ensuring that America would continue to spend more than it produced.

In sum, a tax on imports is, in effect, a tax on exports, both directly by raising the cost of inputs – stifling innovation through competition and prompting retaliation and a general worsening of trade conditions – and indirectly, by currency appreciation and by permitting wage increases in the import-competing industries, which then spill over to the economy at large.

At this point, two broad and related observations can be made about the nature of the gains from trade, each rather counter-intuitive and each of recurring importance. The first is that, although comparative advantage is a dynamic thing that can be acquired through skills upgrading, to benefit fully from trade a country needs to stop doing things in which it has a comparative disadvantage. The second observation is that, despite the economic gains that come from exports, the main benefits of trade for a country come from the improvements in domestic productivity and resource allocation that import competition brings. As Gary Banks, the former head of the Australian Productivity Commission, has pointed out, a country's own barriers to trade generally have a more distorting effect on economic efficiency and incentives to innovate than the trade barriers of other countries (Banks 2003).

But exports do matter, and blocking them, as a weapon of trade, brings harm by encouraging the search for substitutes and by reducing opportunities for growth – opportunities that arise when a firm – particularly one close to the technological frontier – can, via exports, operate in a bigger and more competitive market. And though it is firms, and customers, that feel the brunt, it tends to be governments that pull the strings.

Governments' misguided pursuit of advantage

Our discussion of the four uses of the trade weapon can be seen as falling within the broad framework of economic diplomacy, in which, as Nicholas Bayne and Stephen Woolcock (2017) point out, non-state actors engage, both by shaping government policies and as independent players, but which is nevertheless something that governments do. To that extent, the discussion can also be seen as falling within the debate generated by the innovative work of Henry Farrell and Abraham Newman on weaponized interdependence, whereby a state actor can exploit its position to gain a bargaining advantage over others.[13] It follows that the trade weapon is wielded essentially by the big players, though with repercussions affecting all trading nations.

Each of the four campaigns of trade weaponry discussed here can thus be seen as examples of how governments intervene in, mostly, private markets with the aim of compelling policy change to their perceived advantage. In fact – to repeat – use of the trade weapon, with the attendant risks of protectionist capture and retaliation, yields no net advantage; it is bad for growth and development and either ineffective or counterproductive in the pursuit of other goals. Fortunately – as we will see – there are better ways than unalloyed reliance on the trade weapon.

1
Sanctioning Aggression

Despite twenty years of sanctions imposed on his country, North Korea's Kim Jong-un can now make a nuclear strike anywhere within the United States, and in November 2022 he supplied infantry rockets and missiles to Russia's private military group, Wagner. With Russia itself, an unprecedented campaign of trade and financial sanctions, aimed at crippling the world's eleventh biggest economy, may have helped deny Vladimir Putin the early victory he expected when invading Ukraine in February 2022 but failed to change his behaviour. We thus have a paradox underlying trade sanctions: they generally command support within sender countries, yet tend not to work, while imposing a cost on the sender. Fortunately, as we shall see, there are ways of making sanctions more effective. For while the self-harm endured by sanctioning countries can rightly be seen as a fair price to pay for the goals sought, it is even better if the duration of that harm can be shortened by making sanctions more expeditious.

Trade sanctions are not new. In ancient Greece, the Athenians banned merchants from nearby Megara as a result of tensions over land use and so helped trigger the Peloponnesian War. The context, however, is new, making sanctions both more costly and more likely.

Sanctions have become more costly, as ubiquitous global supply chains magnify the impact of disruption. Indeed, the sanctions on Russia, together with Russia's own countermeasures, are the most compelling example of the trade weapon that could be imagined. They have been characterized as representing no less than a new era of twenty-first-century conflict. And sanctions have become more likely as geostrategic tensions mount and support for unfettered trade weakens. The average number of imposed sanctions over the years 2010 to 2019 almost doubled, to 482 per year from an average of about 250 sanctions per year in the 1990s and 2000s, as what has been dubbed a Cold Trade War became entrenched.[1]

Trade sanctions are also a key element in the vicious circle at the core of this book and have thus been chosen to start our unfolding story.

Sanctions and domestic support: the players and their aims

To set the scene, let's see what sanctions are aimed at, by whom and with what support within sender countries – and how these factors have been changing in recent years, with the advent of new players and new tools.

In a comprehensive study, Gary Hufbauer, Jeffrey Schott, Kimberley Ann Elliott and Barbara Oegg, all of the Peterson Institute for International Economics, have analysed 174 cases of economic sanctions over the period 1914–2000 (Hufbauer et al. 2009). They define sanctions as the deliberate government-inspired withdrawal or threat of withdrawal of customary trade or financial relations. With the spreading importance of trade in financial services, much 'financial' activity can now be legitimately regarded as 'trade' and, therefore, an aspect of the trade weapon. From the data compiled by Gary Hufbauer and his colleagues we can see that the focus of sanctions (between 1914 and 2000) was on three broad areas: military (limiting military action, impairing economic capability and strengthening nuclear safeguards), roughly 40 per cent; improved human rights, 25 per cent; and, often related, regime change, 30 per cent.

Sanctions activity was aimed at a remarkably large and diverse range of sovereign states – slightly over one hundred countries being the object of sanctions on one or more occasion. The senders were more concentrated – twenty-five in total.

The United States has been, and remains, the dominant sender. Since the 1990s, however, three other parties have become more active players: the European Union, Russia and China (Hufbauer and Jung 2020). Between 2004 and 2015, the EU introduced over forty sanctions against twenty-seven states, including Nicaragua (human rights violations), North Korea (nuclear proliferation) and Russia (annexation of foreign territory).

From the 1990s, Russia itself, denied direct control over its former satellites, turned to aggressive diplomacy towards the 'near abroad', with economic sanctions on Estonia and Latvia (via restrictions on oil and gas exports) in response to alleged discrimination against Russian minorities. As a harbinger of things to come, from 2014, responding to US and EU sanctions for the invasion of Crimea, Russia imposed travel bans and food embargoes on the two senders, as well as energy and food embargoes on Ukraine as a counter to its own sanctions on Russia.

China, under Xi Jinping, has conspicuously reversed Deng Xiaoping's guiding principle of non-interference in the affairs of other countries by adopting a more assertive, indeed coercive, style of engagement dubbed Wolf Warrior Diplomacy, after an ultra-nationalistic blockbuster film series. This has involved imposing trade sanctions on a range of targets, including Norway, for awarding the 2010 Nobel Peace Prize to the Chinese dissident Liu Xiaobo, and South Korea, for installing a US-designed defensive missile system.

For its part, the United Nations, which imposed sanctions only four times in its first two decades (1945–65), has done so more than forty times since then.

As well as bringing in additional key players, the twenty-first century has also brought a new dimension to sanctions in the form of targeted cyber-attacks. In the United States, up to and including the Barack Obama administration, the national security adviser and the Pentagon eschewed offensive use of cyber capabilities. However, in a classified executive order, President Donald Trump reversed that policy, opening the possibility of offensive cyber-attacks in future economic sanctions episodes. Media reports indicate that cyber measures have subsequently been deployed against Russia (its electrical grid) and Iran (its financial system).

One thing that has not changed, however, is the dominance of sanctions activity by major powers. Sanctions are a big power phenomenon. Even collective action such as that of the allies against Germany and Japan in the Second World War or the UN against Iraq in 1990 are usually episodes of major powers enlisting their smaller allies.

As an exercise of power, the ultimate objective of the sanction – and the criterion on which its success must be judged – is to change the behaviour of the target country. In pursuing this objective, however, as Hufbauer and his colleagues (2009) point out, the sanction sends a triple message: to the target country it says the sender does not condone the target's actions; to allies it says that words will be supported by deeds; and to domestic audiences it says that the sender government will act to safeguard the nation's vital interests and values. This domestic dimension is particularly important and may also contain an element of quenching a public thirst for retribution, as with the US, European and Japanese sanctions against China in the wake of the Tiananmen massacres.

Three other, relatively recent, developments contribute to the likelihood of broad public support within sender countries (80 per cent of EU citizens polled in June 2022)[2] for the imposition of trade sanctions, at least at the outset.

The first is a heightened public aversion to armed conflict in the wake of experience in Iraq, Afghanistan and Somalia. For while few would now agree with US President Woodrow Wilson that 'apply this economic, peaceful, silent, deadly remedy and there will be no need for force',[3] the use of sanctions – in conjunction with targeted military support

– can nevertheless be presented as reducing the need for sender countries to engage in all-out warfare. This has clearly been a driving motivation for sanctions against Russia's invasion of Ukraine in February 2022 – to trigger a liquidity and balance of payments crisis, making it hard, it was hoped, for Russia to finance the war. A second factor helping explain broad public support for sanctions is the sense of moral engagement – often expressed through 'civil society' and social media – in human rights issues associated with, for example, the treatment of the Uyghur minority in China or the Rohingya in Myanmar. And the third factor contributing to public support within sender countries for the imposition of economic sanctions is the widespread perception of the negative effects of globalization and a corresponding tolerance of measures that serve to restrain it.

Yet, despite this support, sanctions tend not to work. Let's see why.

Why sanctions fail: market power, the burden of pain and conflict expectations

According to the extensive review undertaken by Gary Hufbauer and his colleagues (2009), only about one out of three sanctions cases since the Second World War (and up to 2000) succeeded in achieving their stated goal of changing the target's behaviour. Why is this? As a rough rule of thumb, sanctions are likely to fail (in changing the target's behaviour) if some combination of three conditions applies. These are:

- when the target country is able, through market power, to sidestep sanctions, particularly if unilateral, while imposing considerable economic pain on the sender;
- when the target country – likely in the history of sanctions to be authoritarian – has a high pain threshold and a correspondingly large capacity to withstand sanctions;
- when the target country has a high expectation of continuing tension with the sender and is therefore reluctant to make concessions, under sanctions pressure, that would

compromise future negotiating flexibility. This element is central to the *conflict expectations model* developed by Daniel Drezner (1999).[4]

Before we come to our Russia–Ukraine story, two case studies are particularly pertinent in throwing light on how these three factors play out: the sanctions regimes applied in response to nuclear programmes on the Korean peninsula and the use of sanctions to limit Iran's nuclear weapons programme.

Nuclear programmes on the Korean peninsula: two contrasting sanctions cases and the lessons to be drawn

South Korea (1969–76)

The decision of the Republic of Korea (ROK) to start a nuclear weapons programme was triggered by the announcement of the Nixon doctrine in July 1969. Under the doctrine, the United States would honour all treaty commitments and secure its vital interests, but 'in cases involving other types of aggression, the United States would furnish military and economic assistance when requested and appropriate, but nations directly threatened should assume primary responsibility for their own defence.'[5]

In 1970, the United States had 63,000 troops stationed in the ROK, with approximately 600 tactical nuclear weapons. President Nixon proposed to withdraw a third of the troops. The South Korean prime minister, Chung Il-kwon, captured the ROK's dilemma: 'We are not against the Nixon Doctrine in principle, but if North Korean [leader] Kim Il Sung miscalculates, the South Korean people will wonder if America will abandon its security treaty or come to our defence.'[6]

In response to this uncertainty, ROK President Park Chung Hee set up the Weapons Exploitation Committee, which, in the early 1970s, voted unanimously to develop nuclear weapons. By 1975, Seoul had secured the three prerequisites for a viable nuclear programme: sufficient technical knowledge, a missile delivery vehicle (the Nike

Hercules surface-to-air missile) and the promise of access to weapons-grade nuclear fuel via a deal being negotiated with France for the provision of a radioactive-waste reprocessing plant.

These developments prompted a series of US sanctions against the ROK, including the threat to halt all trade involving Seoul's civilian nuclear energy programme and military procurement and the termination of loan guarantees from the Export–Import Bank worth $227 million if the reprocessing plant deal was not cancelled.

In January 1976, South Korea cancelled plans to purchase the reprocessing plant and abandoned its nuclear weapons programme. This reversal was widely seen as being the result of US sanctions pressure. The US Office of Technology Assessment wrote that 'Recent American pressure upon South Korea to forgo acquisition of a reprocessing plant illustrates that sanctions can be effective, at least in a situation where the target state is highly vulnerable.'[7]

Experience with North Korea has been very different.

North Korea (1987–present)

The development of nuclear weapons by the Democratic People's Republic of Korea (DPRK) was given a major boost by the end of the Cold War and the collapse of its privileged trading relationship with Russia and China. Both countries now insisted on hard currency payments for the energy and grain imports on which the DPRK economy depended. The North Korean economy shrank. And when Soviet Foreign Minister Eduard Shevardnadze went to Pyongyang in 1990 to inform the DPRK leadership of Russia's decision to recognize South Korea, the DPRK responded by threatening to develop nuclear weapons. Pyongyang would have been mindful of the recent demise of its close ally East Germany and had no wish to be absorbed by the ROK.

Shortly afterwards, the United States detected an explosion at Yongbyon, consistent with a blast necessary to detonate a nuclear device. By 1994, the DPRK had test-fired its Rodong-1 missile, which had the range to strike western Japan. There followed a lengthy period in which the response of the US and other interested parties was a mix of carrots and sticks.

In October 1991 President Bush announced the withdrawal of nuclear weapons from the ROK. In October 1994 a Framework Agreement was signed between the US and the DPRK – essentially offering economic inducements – North Korea was to freeze activity at its nuclear facilities and the US would provide heavy oil in lieu of lost energy from reactors. America also sought to promote sanctions in the UN but had no bilateral trade to make it effective, and China, Russia, Japan and South Korea all preferred negotiation to sanctions.

Meanwhile, DPRK nuclear weapons activities continued. In 1993 it had withdrawn from both the Treaty on the Non-Proliferation of Nuclear Weapons and the International Atomic Energy Agency.

Critical early moves to sanctions came in 2005 – with action against Banco Delta Asia, in possession of $25 million of the ruling Kim family fortune, and with China cutting off supplies of heating oil. In 2006, UN sanctions were imposed through UNSCR 1718, targeting the DPRK's primary export industry and broader links to the international economy. The US, Japan and South Korea also imposed their own sanctions regimes, including a Japanese prohibition of ships entering its ports that had previously visited North Korea. This pressure may have contributed to Pyongyang's willingness to negotiate an agreement with the US, China, Japan, Russia and the ROK; the 'Six Party Talks' led to an undertaking to dismantle North Korea's nuclear facilities in 2007. Nevertheless, none of this was, in the words of Richard Nephew (2018), 'sufficient to moderate N[orth] K[orea]'s actual activities of concern'. Subsequently, North Korea boasted of having developed thermonuclear weapons and a missile-deployable nuclear warhead with a capacity to attack adversaries as far away as the West Coast of the United States.

Another twist came in February 2019, with a meeting in Hanoi between presidents Kim Jong-un and Donald Trump at which Kim sought sanctions relief, offering in return to dismantle his main nuclear complex (at Yongbyon). Talks stalled with Trump's apparent loss of interest. Subsequently,

North Korea, increasingly impatient with lack of sanctions relief from America, has revived its ties with its Cold War partners, while accelerating the scope and sophistication of its nuclear and missile capabilities.

On 8 September 2022, Kim Jong-un, at a ceremony marking the seventy-fourth anniversary of the founding of the DPRK, announced a new law that rendered the development of the country's nuclear weapons force 'irreversible', precluded any negotiation on denuclearization, and enumerated five scenarios under which 'automatic and immediate' use of the nuclear weapon would be justified. Among those scenarios would be an exchange of missile fire such as occurred in 2017.[8]

In October 2022, the DPRK was among just four countries that voted against the UN General Assembly resolution condemning Russia's 'attempted illegal annexation' of four Ukrainian regions. And, in November 2022, the DPRK supplied infantry rockets and missiles to Russia's private military group Wagner, in violation of UN Security Council resolutions.

Critically, the deadlock with North Korea carries the risk of intensified DPRK cyber disruption, as Pyongyang deploys its estimated 7,000 highly trained 'cyber warriors'. Deadlock also raises the spectre of regional nuclear proliferation, with 70 per cent of the South Korean population supporting the development of a national nuclear capability.[9]

Over twenty years of experience suggests that inflicting pain on North Korea – which can now make a nuclear strike anywhere within the United States – does not engender a change of behaviour.

In the case of the Korean peninsula, all three factors outlined above would help explain the success of sanctions against the ROK: relatively low costs incurred by the sender, a democratic regime in Seoul, and low expectation of future conflict between sender and target. In the case of the DPRK, however, two of the negative factors are clearly present: a high expectation of future conflict and a highly autocratic regime in the target country.[10] With China and Russia likely to oppose any strengthening of sanctions, some combination of carrots and sticks may offer the only way out of what is a highly dangerous and seemingly intractable situation.

If the expectation is that trade sanctions are more likely to be aimed at aggressive behaviour by autocratic targets with whom tension and conflict is likely than at aggressive behaviour by democratically run allies, then there will be a matching expectation that, overall, sanctions are unlikely to succeed. This expectation tends to be borne out with our second case study – the Iran nuclear programme.

Iran nuclear sanctions: beware unintended consequences

Experience with Iran nuclear sanctions is instructive because it shows what can happen under a discontinuous sanctions regime. It also illustrates the power of unintended consequences. The sequence of events is briefly as follows.

In 2018 the Trump administration withdrew from the 2015 Joint Comprehensive Plan of Action (JCPOA), brokered by America plus China, France, Germany, Russia and the UK, effectively reimposing sanctions – notably on Iranian oil exports. In response, Tehran returned to rapid expansion of its nuclear programme and doubled down on its ballistic-missiles programme and regional trouble making, including attacks on Saudi Arabia and allied troops in Iraq.

To counter the secondary sanctions against non-US firms doing business with Iran, in 2020, France, Germany and the UK created the 'Instrument for Supporting Trade Exchanges' (INSTEX) to help EU firms trade with Tehran and facilitate non-US dollar transactions. This lessened the already small likelihood that Iran would abandon its nuclear goals. This pattern continued when it appeared, in early 2021, that the administration of President Joe Biden would not return to the deal – that is, would continue with sanctions. Tehran rapidly expanded its uranium enrichment programme to 60 per cent, coming dangerously close to producing weapons-grade uranium.

Then the reversal. As of late August 2022, the Biden administration (in bilateral talks with Iran mediated by the EU) was close to renewing the JCPOA (effectively ending sanctions). In response, Iran would agree to give up its stockpile of higher-level enriched uranium, remove thousands of advanced centrifuges from operation, and cease to have a pathway to a plutonium-based nuclear weapon. It would also be fully open to intrusive International Atomic Energy Agency inspections.

Behind the scenes, one important unintended consequence that helped ensure the failure of the sanctions regime was that the effect of the resumption of sanctions under the Trump administration was simply to force much of Iran's oil trade underground, allowing the Islamic Revolutionary Guards Corps (IRGC) to sell its own share of oil and build economic conglomerates. As a result, the bulk of IRGC income sat outside the official government budget. In addition, Iran has been able to sell oil to China, marked as coming from Malaysia, Oman or the United Arab Emirates.

In terms of our criteria for sanctions failure, two were clearly present under the resumed sanctions in the form of a target government with both a high expectation of future conflict and a marked capacity to avoid at least some of the cost of the sanctions regime.

In the case of Iran nuclear, one would have to say that sanctions appear to have been counterproductive – (apart from a possible back-handed strength via the promise of their removal).

Consistent with that view, it has indeed been suggested, by Trita Parsi, that the best way of making the renewed plan stick (and avoiding another Republican withdrawal in 2025) would be to build confidence by *further* dismantling sanctions by extending the sanctions-removal to primary sanctions – that is, by allowing a resumption of *direct* US–Iran trade (beyond the removal of secondary sanctions involving only trade with third parties).[11]

Sanctions experience on the Korean peninsula and with Iran is broadly supportive of our three criteria for sanctions success. Let's see how they measure up in the case of sanctions against Russia for its invasion of Ukraine in 2022.

Sanctions against Russia for the invasion of Ukraine: not the key factor

On the basis of their analysis of economic sanctions imposed in the period 1914–2000, Gary Hufbauer and his colleagues

(2009) concluded that the cost imposed by sanctions on target countries represents barely a ripple in the world economy. In 2000, the annual cost of all ongoing sanctions represented only 0.4 per cent of total world exports. Nevertheless, looking at the costs imposed on target and senders by the sanctions imposed on Russia for its invasion of Ukraine in February 2022, it is clear that the pain is far from negligible. The scale of the sanctions together with the size of the Russian economy and the extent of its integration into world energy and grain markets have added a new dimension to the sanctions calculus.

Sanctions on and by Russia, by dramatically raising the cost of energy, have dealt a severe blow to the economies of low- and middle-income countries, while Russia's initial blockade of grain shipments out of Ukraine exacerbated a growing world food crisis.[12]

In terms of sanctions effectiveness, the three determinants identified here for success were never going to be propitious in the case of Russia–Ukraine. Vladimir Putin had a high expectation of future conflict and a corresponding aversion to conceding ground. The capacity of the Russian people to bear pain – and to be shielded from the truth[13] – was demonstrably high. According to the *Washington Post*, the Russian defence minister, Sergei Shoigu, told the British government in February 2021 that Russians 'can suffer like no one else'.[14] And, given its dominant place in global food and energy markets, Russia's ability to bypass sanctions while imposing collateral damage was always going to be a key factor.

Reflecting on the economic impact of the war in Ukraine, OECD Secretary General Mathias Cormann observed that the aim of the sanctions against Russia was to 'maximize pressure on Russia while causing minimal disruption in the countries introducing them.'[15] That of course is the key. As we look at the Ukraine sanctions story from different angles, a recurring theme will be the porous nature of the sanctions regime.

Partial sanctions enforcement
The dominant market role of Russia led to the widely shared view that 'the biggest flaw (in sanctions effectiveness) is that

full or partial embargoes are not being enforced by over 100 countries with 40 per cent of world GDP.'[16] Thus, after six months of sanctions, Dubai was brimming with Russian cash, and you could fly with Emirates and other companies to Moscow seven times a day. Russian diamonds were still trading in Antwerp, Belgium.

Urals oil was flowing to Asia: to China, where Igor Sechin, the boss of Russia's state-owned oil giant Rosneft, had struck big oil-supply agreements with China National Petroleum Corporation, and to India, where Rosneft used its part ownership of Nayara Energy to gain a toe hold on one of the world's fastest growing consumer markets. It was thus estimated that Russia would be able to redirect 75 per cent of the oil that Europe shunned.

Japan was also a challenge for sanctions compliance. Archipelagic Japan has no pipelines or electricity grids linking it to other countries. It is the world's second biggest importer of liquefied natural gas (LNG), and some 9 per cent of its supply comes from Russia. It was estimated that, in 2022, some 50 to 70 per cent of Sakhalin's gas output would have headed for Japan. While Japan had joined the sanctions effort, Prime Minister Kishida Fumio was silent on Russian gas.

EU sanctions did not apply to the 40 per cent of its uranium imports coming from Russia and Kazakhstan to fuel nuclear power plants in France, Finland, Hungary and Slovakia.

After six months of sanctions, the US was still trying to convince its allies to impose a price cap on Russian oil – rises in which were negating the effects of volume controls. And no embargo was planned on Russian gas, which was harder to replace. Banks that process Europe's vast purchases of Russian fuel, notably Gazprombank, were still being allowed to use SWIFT.

The combined effects of energy leakages meant that, in the critical first one hundred days of its invasion of Ukraine, Russia earned $97 billion in revenues from oil and gas, according to the Centre for Research on Energy and Clean Air (a Finnish think tank). This was more than enough to pay for its expenditure on the war, estimated at $876 million a day.

Nine months after the invasion – though sanctions, together with Western military aid and the tenacity of Ukrainian forces, had prevented the easy victory Vladimir Putin had hoped for – oil money continued to flow into Putin's war chest. Hence the decision that, from 5 December 2022, the G7, the EU plus Australia would ban the import of seaborne Russian crude oil and stop their firms from insuring, shipping or trading Russian oil, unless – as demanded by America – that oil was sold at a price below a cap set by the West. The cap, though resourceful, served only to highlight the persisting sanctions conundrum – how to harm Russia without reducing global oil supply and fuelling inflation. Predictably, Russia responded to the price cap by announcing an oil export ban on the countries applying it.

After two months of operation of the price cap, supporters claimed success, given data suggesting this crude was being sold at a 38 per cent discount. Unfortunately, this was not so, as Russian crude was simply diverted to India and China, which do not share pricing information. At the same time, Russia found new sources of shipping and finance infrastructure, with Europe's share falling from a half to 36 per cent.

The nature of the sanctions conundrum was further exposed when, in November 2022, the United States was obliged to relax sanctions against Venezuelan oil because of the global energy crunch.

As well as energy considerations, global food supply was a constraint on the implementation of sanctions. In July 2022, the United States and the European Union, in the face of a growing cereal shortage on world markets, each agreed to unblock Russian funds under sanction in Western banks in order to permit the financing of Russian wheat exports.[17] The situation was particularly acute on the continent of Africa, which was facing a 45 per cent increase in the price of its wheat imports, close to half of which it sources from Russia and Ukraine. In November 2022, the governments of the United States, the EU and Britain were obliged to issue a statement saying that the sanctions target was Russia's war machine, not its food and fertilizer industry. But revenue from food and fertilizer is fungible! And the regulatory complexity of the sanctions regime presented its own challenge. In 2022, an Australian logistics firm, Toll Holdings, was found by the US Office of Foreign Assets Control to have breached US laws against sanctioned groups 2,958 times. The company, which was found to have sent thousands of shipments, valued at $48.4 million, to or from sanctioned countries in contravention of US law, claimed a misunderstanding about the regulations relating to payments through the US financial system for otherwise permissible shipments.[18]

The persisting difficulty in the case of sanctions against Russia was that many of the Russian entities targeted were much bigger, more complex and more deeply embedded in global business networks than previous targets in, say, Iran, Myanmar, North Korea or Syria.

Another way of assessing sanctions effectiveness is to examine more closely the relative impact on sender and target. Looking at the contrasting experience of the EU, as a major sender and Russia-dependent entity, and Russia itself, the complexity of the sanctions fallout is clearly evident.

The impact on Europe

After six months of conflict and sanctions, in early September 2022 the EU was preparing to boycott most Russian oil. For its part, however, Russia, in retaliation, had halted gas supplies to Europe through its biggest pipeline, Nord Stream 1, initially citing maintenance[19] and then, on 5 September, saying the pipeline would be shut down as long as Western sanctions were in place. At this point, EU gas prices were nine times higher than a year earlier, and, according to Bruegel, a Brussels-based think tank, European governments had spent €280 billion in the preceding months to cushion the shock.

The risk of a gas crunch point was always evident. Gas satisfied a quarter of EU energy demand, and Russia supplied a third of that. Unlike oil and coal, which are fungible and globally traded, gas must either be piped or transported as LNG using facilities that take years to construct. There was also a highly asymmetric dependence – and corresponding sanctions vulnerability – on the gas market between the EU and Russia. While gas was crucial to the EU economy, it represented only 2 per cent of Russia's GDP.

Energy response measures in Europe ranged over reduced fuel taxes, cuts to Value Added Tax, customer subsidies, retail price caps, universal cash transfers – and a massive increase in imports of coal, the price of which hit three records in the nine months to September 2022. The EU Commission began working on limiting the price of electricity by decoupling it from the cost of gas – in effect extending the subsidy scheme pioneered by Portugal and Spain to the whole bloc. Notwithstanding these measures, the EU officially went into recession at the end of 2022. In the meantime, inflation – also in part the result of rising energy prices – had put an end to the era of free borrowing.[20]

Let's see how this impact on Europe compares with that on Russia itself.

The impact on Russia
The action taken against Russia lifts sanctions to a new level – aimed at crippling the world's eleventh biggest economy. After six months of conflict and sanctions, imports had collapsed by 22 per cent (WTO 2022), half of Russia's $580 billion currency reserves lay frozen, and most of its big banks were cut off from the global payments system and the SWIFT messaging network.[21]

The US was no longer buying Russian oil, and an EU oil embargo was foreshadowed. Russian firms were barred from buying inputs, from engines to semiconductors, with US chip sales to Russia down 90 per cent in the year to September 2022 – hindering new plastic card issuance on MIR, the domestic payment system. Russian airlines were banned from North Atlantic airspace. And oligarchs and officials faced travel bans and asset freezes. It was estimated that some 1,500 members of Russia's kleptocratic elite were unable to travel to some or all Western countries.

On a three-year horizon, isolation from Western markets was expected to create havoc, with a fifth of civil aircraft grounded and upgrades to telecom networks seriously compromised. As an indirect effect of the sanctions, it was estimated by Konstantin Sonin of the University of Chicago that several hundreds of thousands of Russians – many of them highly skilled – had left the country since the invasion. But, after six months of sanctions, a knockout blow had not materialized. In the course of 2022, IMF estimates of the expected fall in Russian GDP were progressively lowered from 15, then to 8.5, then to 3.4 per cent – eventually realizing a fall of 2.2 per cent in 2022. And energy sales were expected to generate a $265 billion current account surplus in 2022. According to a respected Russia watcher, Chris Weafer, the economy was not collapsing. Throughout, Russia was able to maintain its military spending.

This somewhat indeterminate outcome results from the complex and contradictory effects of sanctions. The contradiction is nicely captured by Nicholas Mulder in an essay for *Foreign Affairs* when he points out that, while Russian tanks were running on microchips cannibalized from washing machines, trade data showed a 241 per cent year-on-year increase in Chinese chip exports to Russia (Mulder 2022c).

Whatever the final outcome of Vladimir Putin's invasion of Ukraine in February 2022, it was predestined that the credits would go to the courage and skill of the Ukrainian forces and to the massive military support provided by America and Europe – not to the sanctions regime.

China as a sanctions target: the case of the Uyghur

If the three criteria for success were never going to be propitious in the case of sanctions against Russia for its invasion of Ukraine, this is even more the case when looking at sanctions against China. China's place in the global economy is significantly more important than that of Russia; the Chinese people, zero-COVID dissatisfaction notwithstanding, have a high pain threshold – though not an unlimited one;[22] and

Xi Jinping's world view is predicated on the assumption of future conflict.

No case better shows the difficulty of making trade sanctions work than action against the abuse of the Uyghur minority in Xinjiang. Despite years of mounting evidence of a violent campaign of incarceration and forced indoctrination of the Uyghur ethnic minority in Xinjiang, it took three years – until December 2021 – to complete the report of the former UN human rights chief Michelle Bachelet. The report was then delayed a further nine months, including by a request from the Chinese authorities that it come out after the Winter Olympics in February 2022 (at which China appointed a Uyghur athlete to carry the Olympic torch).

When it was finally released, on 31 August 2022, the report was blunt in its appraisal, concluding that China's actions 'may constitute international crimes, in particular, crimes against humanity.' Appalling accounts of abuse, including rape and torture, at the detention centres in Xinjiang were affirmed. In a 131-page response, China justified some of its actions on security grounds and said the report was 'based on disinformation'. It is clearly very difficult to establish an authoritative, international account of human rights abuses. It is equally difficult to impose effective sanctions against such abuses.

In June 2021, G7 leaders, mindful of the Uyghur dilemma, stated their common concern over forced labour in supply chains, 'including in the agricultural, solar, and garment sectors', all areas of activity in Xinjiang. Later that year, American government agencies, among them the State, Treasury and Commerce departments, formally advised businesses with supply chains in China of the risks for those with investments there. Japanese businesses were also warned by the government to be careful about supply chains through the area. And the EU began work on due diligence legislation, obliging firms to check that their operations and suppliers are not engaged in human rights abuses.

Subsequently, Western legislation has firmed up. From mid-2021, a new law in Germany required firms with more than 3,000 employees to prove by 2023 that their supply chains were free of human-rights abuses. Penalties for infraction can be 2 per cent of a company's annual revenue. In the United States, the Uyghur Forced Labour Prevention Act, which passed into law in December 2021, bans imports of products from the region of Xinjiang on the assumption that they are made with the forced labour of Uyghurs. Goods from Xinjiang can be brought into America only if importers can prove that forced labour was not used in their production.

In some cases, it will be relatively straightforward to identify products made by forced labour. For example, bans have been imposed on imports from a Xinjiang-based company that produces the type of silicon needed for solar cells. But how do you locate the fibres within a Chinese manufactured fabric or garment as coming – or not – from forced labour in Xinjiang? China, which accounts for about 40 per cent of the world's textile exports, denies the existence of forced labour and does not allow proper inspection of supply chains in the region. And some of the more specialist products from Xinjiang will not be banned – for example, the nitrogen heterocyclic compounds used in cancer drugs.

Then of course there is the ultimate test: even if the sanctions can be made operative, they will not necessarily achieve the end goal of changing the behaviour of the target – in this case, China's mistreatment of its Uyghur minority. Indeed, part of China's response to sanctions has been to apply counter-measures to firms involved – as with sanctions placed on H&M for refusing to buy cotton from Xinjiang.

This is not a counsel of despair, but it does suggest that sanctions – as well as being as sharply and expeditiously executed as possible – may also need to be accompanied by more classic diplomacy.

Sanctions effectiveness: summing up

To sum up, it would seem that the chances of the trade weapon in the form of sanctions changing a target's behaviour are quite slim. Close observation by Daniel Drezner and Bruce Jentleson suggests that American sanctions – still by far the most common – have been more effective in imposing economic costs than in converting that impact into policy change (Jentleson 2022; Drezner 2021).[23] This would seem to be a broadly applicable conclusion, regardless of whether the channel of influence is deterrence, retribution or rehabilitation.

Deterrence: Sanctions on Russia for the annexation of Crimea in 2014 did not deter Vladimir Putin from invading Ukraine in February 2022. Sanctions by China on Taiwan did not prevent the pro-independence candidate winning the presidency in 2016 and being re-elected four years later. And, as we have seen, North Korea's nuclear weapons programme, sanctions notwithstanding, proceeds with even more vigour.

Retribution: The revocation of US visas of Saudis connected with the assassination of Jared Khashoggi did not bring the instigators to justice or prompt any acknowledgement of culpability on the part of the Saudi governing regime.

Rehabilitation: Human rights abuses in Myanmar and Xinjiang stubbornly persist, regardless of the sanctions being imposed.

So, to repeat, if on balance sanctions are more likely to be imposed on authoritarian adversaries with high conflict expectations and pain thresholds such that the chances of the sanctions changing the behaviour of the target are probably quite slim, the inevitable question arises: Can things be done differently?

A better way: some implications for policy makers

Neither resignation in the face of aggression nor all-out military conflict – with a clear risk of nuclear engagement – is likely to be seen as a viable alternative to sanctions (plus selective military assistance). As Bruce Jentleson (2022) has observed, sanctions are here to stay. The question then is, rather: Can sanctions be made to work more effectively?

For while the self-harm endured by sanctioning countries can rightly be seen as the just price to pay for the normative gains in social and political freedom sought by sanctions, it is still better if the duration of that harm can be shortened by making sanctions more expeditious.

Following our rule of thumb, sanctions are more likely to be effective the more policy makers are able to ensure maximum target pain and minimal sender pain; give target citizens a voice; and remove or reduce the target's expectation of future conflict.

Distributing the pain

From the sender's point of view, sanctions need to impose the maximum disruption on the target in the shortest possible time[24] while minimizing self-harm. Reducing self-harm means resisting protectionist capture within the sanctions regime. It also means bringing flexibility and resilience to sectors that may be dependent on target-country suppliers. This is nowhere more pressing than in the European energy market.

Europe needs to bring greater resilience to its energy supply. This can be done in several ways, including through common purchases of LNG cargoes; the construction of, conspicuously lacking, import terminals for LNG; shared storage capacity between countries; and guaranteed free movement of gas. A step in the right direction was taken in December 2022, when Germany opened its first LNG vessel, a floating storage and regasification unit (FSRU) at Wilhelmshaven on the North Sea coast for this vital transition fuel. This is to be the first of several FSRUs, aimed to permit by the end of 2023 the importation of 30 billion cubic metres of gas – well over half the volume of the gas previously flowing from Russia to Germany before Vladimir Putin – in retaliation against sanctions – cut off supplies.

More broadly, there is scope for greater digitalization of energy-related stock management, a common hierarchy governing rationing across the EU, with intensive energy users impacted first and private consumers last, and a coherent continent-wide energy security mechanism. Such a mechanism would help the transition to cleaner energy, shaking off what Claudia Kemfert of the German Institute for Economic Research calls a gas-fuelled 'illusion of competitiveness'.

Giving target citizens a voice

In the case of the tensions with Moscow, bridges need to remain open with Russia's intelligentsia. As the political commentator Henry Ergas has pointed out, 'from Pushkin to Pasternak and Akhmatova, the brightest jewels of Russia's heritage have always stressed, with Dostoevsky, that "while tyranny is a habit capable of being developed and which at last becomes a disease, man is an odd creature who would prefer to be flayed alive rather than surrender his freedom."' Keeping that message alive should be a priority for the West, and to boycott Russia's writers and artists would be a grave error.[25]

In practical terms, scope exists to bypass censorship within Russia by giving help to the roughly 500 exiled Russian journalists reporting on the war from cities such as Riga, Tbilisi, Vilnius and Berlin, as well as assistance to the VPN services used by nearly half of young Russians. Foreign-sourced funding, via grants from charities, is particularly important, as both MasterCard and Visa block Russian transactions outside Russia.

Reducing the target's expectation of conflict: carrots and sticks

Reducing the expectation that future conflict is unavoidable is likely to require sanctioning governments – preferably acting multilaterally – to combine sanctions activity (and the concomitant prospect of sanctions relief) with classic diplomacy; to use carrots as well as sticks.[26] The goal is not to resolve all differences – as Joseph Nye (2004) has pointed out, interdependence does not mean harmony – but, rather, to create an element of trust and an expectation that differences can be managed and outright physical conflict avoided.

An example of how a combination of carrot and stick can work is provided by the squeeze on Libya by America and its allies in the early 2000s, when a mix of sanctions plus financial inducements persuaded Muammar Gaddafi to end his weapons of mass destruction programme and stop funding terrorism. Carrots of multilateral diplomatic flexibility, together with a clear commitment to sanctions relief when agreed benchmarks are met, must be part of negotiations to end four particularly egregious contemporary acts of aggression.

Russia–Ukraine: A commitment by Ukraine and its Western allies that Ukraine will remain a neutral state may be key in ending Russian aggression, but combined with undertakings, called for by the United States and its G7 allies in October 2022, to ensure Ukraine's recovery and reconstruction, to respect the UN Charter's protection of territorial integrity, and to safeguard Ukraine's ability to defend itself in the future, all backed by de-escalation by Russia and negotiation over the territories it seized. Over the longer term, consideration could be given to establishing Ukraine as a trade bridge, with preferential access to both the EU Common Market and Russia's Eurasian Economic Union.[27]

The Uyghur minority in Xinjiang: The provision of multilateral aid flows into the region should continue, but with careful application of due diligence to avoid episodes such as the World Bank's funding of dubious 'vocational schools' in Xinjiang in 2019. Outside auditors could also be appointed to review evidence of forced labour and give the green light, where appropriate, to selected supply chains, such as those involved in producing the nitrogen heterocyclic compounds used in cancer treatment.

North Korea: Kim Jong-un may be susceptible to the provision of humanitarian aid and COVID-19 vaccines, together with a commitment to medium-term Western infrastructure investment in the DPRK for energy and transport network development. This would build on Kim's encouragement of entrepreneurial groups and the deal broached between himself and Donald Trump in 2019.

Taiwan: A basis for averting Chinese aggression may be to combine a carefully articulated condemnation by Western leaders of Chinese attempts at forced reunification together with a clear expression of opposition to unilateral moves by Taiwan towards total independence. Putting the Taiwan case in stark perspective, what would *not* help would be a move to impose pre-emptive sanctions on China that sought to restrict Beijing's access to Taiwanese semiconductors.

The history of conflict sparked by trade sanctions is replete with precedents. Among those in modern times is Japan's attack on Pearl Harbor and entry into the Second World War, triggered in large part by the US oil embargo imposed on the country by President Franklin Roosevelt. Among the earliest examples of sanctions seeding conflict is the embargo placed on Megara by the Athenians, leading to the Peloponnesian War in 431 BC – a reminder that resonates, given recurring talk of a 'Thucydides Trap' as China's growing clout rubs up against the established power of the United States. A semiconductor sanction on China could trigger that trap in a very decisive way (see box 1).[28]

> **Box 1 The UK and the China threat: the perils of a semiconductor sanction**
>
> In September 2022, the UK government announced its intention to redesignate China as a 'threat' rather than simply a 'systemic competitor'. This was consistent with the latest British defence review, which calls China 'the biggest state-based threat' to the country's economic security.
>
> And action goes with the words. The UK government is mandated to remove all Huawei equipment from 5G networks by 2027; it has declined, on security grounds,

a Chinese acquisition of the electronic design software company Pulsic, and was set to block the purchase of Britain's largest semiconductor plant, Newport Wafer Fab, by the Chinese firm Wingtech.

These moves against Beijing are a reflection not only of the expressed security concerns but also of British disquiet over Beijing's treatment of the Uyghur population in Xinjiang, the suppression of democratic rights in Hong Kong, and the exercise of what is seen as 'debt-trap diplomacy' under the Belt and Road Initiative. And then, of course, there is Taiwan. In August 2022, the Foreign Office summoned China's ambassador to the UK, Zheng Zeguang, to explain Beijing's 'aggressive and wide-ranging escalation' in its relations with Taipei.

In taking commercial action against Beijing, the UK government might be expected to draw lessons from Australia's recent quarrels with China, prompted by Canberra's unilateral call for an enquiry into the origins of the COVID-19 pandemic: that, if you want to take on China, better to do so in the company of friends; and that underlying mutual commercial interests can withstand transitory tensions (the vital trade in iron ore between Australia and China has not been fundamentally challenged). The danger of such lessons is of broad strategic disquiet being conflated with action to sanction China in its trade and economic activity in a way that escalates tension and the risk of conflict.

The extreme – though not inconceivable – sanction would be a collectively endorsed, pre-emptive action to limit China's access to Taiwanese semiconductors – in effect, widening the earlier Trump administration sanction preventing the Taiwan Semiconductor Manufacturing Company from supplying Huawei.

The background to this eventuality is the way Washington has steadily ratcheted up restraints on China's ability to develop a domestic chip capacity – limiting (as we will see in the next chapter) the kind of chip-making equipment that US firms can export to China, while enlisting friendly parties, such as Japan's Nikon Corporation and the Netherlands' ASML, to join its technological blockade.

The result is that China is now dependent on Taiwan for 90 per cent of its semiconductors – the lifeblood of China's economy. That dependence creates a vulnerability which, in an albeit extreme scenario, could be exploited by a collectively endorsed chips embargo to which Britain, already subject to US arm-twisting over Huawei and itself upgrading the China 'threat', might be persuaded to subscribe.

Hence the ultimate dilemma: of all the hypotheticals, an embargo on China's access to Taiwanese semiconductors is among the more plausible triggers for a Chinese military attack on Taiwan.

Closing thoughts

Looking ahead, with democracy in decline,[29] sanctions use will not only persist but, rather, in all likelihood, increase. The danger in this situation is that countries – in the anticipation of sanctions activity or in the avoidance of asymmetric interdependence – will seek to reduce their vulnerability via the pursuit of self-sufficiency. Indeed, the historian Nicholas Mulder suggests that, as countries that consider themselves vulnerable to sanctions progressively withdraw from the world economy, their pursuit of autarky and other countries' search for workable sanctions will see them 'locked in an escalatory spiral' (Mulder 2022b). The case for Western leaders, collectively, making multilateral sanctions more expeditious and effective is thus twofold: to help foster peace and human rights, but also to help avoid further weakening of the globalization that has underpinned three decades of international growth and development. We will put a spotlight on that weakening in the next chapter of our story.

2
Arming the Global Value Chain

World leaders, from Emmanuel Macron to Xi Jinping, are calling for their countries to become more self-reliant. At first blush, this looks fair enough. They do so because of growing geostrategic tensions, linked largely to the rise of China and in response to the widespread disruption to global value chains in everything from facemasks to heating oil that has become only too apparent with the COVID-19 pandemic and the war in Ukraine. But the pursuit of self-reliance through weaponized trade – whether by blocked Huawei access to US technology, subsidy-fuelled re-shoring in chip production or ill-advised 'friend-shoring' – while not spelling the end of globalization, is seriously weakening the gains from trade while imposing a hefty, and mounting, bill on taxpayers,[1] starting at €390 billion in Europe and a massive $2 trillion in America.

Fortunately, alternative ways exist of building genuine resilience in dealing with concerns about vulnerability to supply-chain dependence, starting with sound economic management at home.[2] But, first, to set the scene, let's see how the much talked of global value chain actually functions.

How the global value chain works

The fruits of the global value chain (GVC) are ubiquitous in daily life, from the Pfizer COVID-19 vaccine, which requires 280 components from eighty-six suppliers in nineteen countries, to the author's e-bike, assembled in Spain from a frame imported from Taiwan, suspension from the United States and a motor from Japan.

The fragmentation of global production is not new. But the scale of fragmentation under the current period of globalization, or, as Richard Baldwin (2006) calls it, the second unbundling, is unprecedented; over half of global trade is now in intra-industry intermediate goods and services rather than in the exchange of finished products. The geographic separation of various production stages, which started in the 1970s in the United States and Japan, became more attractive in the 1990s with the continuing decline in trade costs on account of the information and communications technology (ICT) revolution, the conclusion of the GATT Uruguay Round, the signing of the General Agreement on Trade in Services, and the wave of preferential trade agreements.

Nevertheless, the momentum of the global supply chain has slowed in recent years, as protectionist forces have put brakes on the gains from trade. According to one recent study, globalization through the GVC actually peaked in 2012, since when supply chains have become more domestic (Miroudot and Nordstrom 2020). This trend – if accentuated – risks further eroding the benefits of international specialization.

Before looking at the threats to the supply chain it is worth briefly examining just how the GVC works. It involves a complex dynamic of often opposing forces.[3]

Agglomeration and dispersion – The New Economic Geography theory launched by Paul Krugman in the 1990s (Krugman 1991) views the locational outcome within the GVC as a balancing of the forces of agglomeration and dispersion. Agglomeration, which generates geographical clustering, is favoured by, for example, knowledge spillovers, supply links or the need to be close to customers. Dispersion forces are governed by opportunities for fragmented specialization, which, in turn, involves movement in opposing directions.

Vertical and horizontal specialization – Vertical specialization is determined by the wage gaps between skilled and unskilled labour and involves the allocation of skill-intensive production to high-wage nations and labour-intensive stages to low-wage nations (reminding us yet again of the continuing relevance of Ricardo's comparative advantage but also, with some refinement, of the Heckscher–Ohlin–Stolper–Samuelson theory). Assembly of the iPhone in China, and now in India, is an example of vertical specialization. Under vertical specialization, firms can minimize the total cost of production by organizing the productive activity into several blocks, each block being produced in the country where marginal cost is the lowest.[4] In contrast, horizontal specialization occurs between high-wage nations and is based not on differing factor prices but on the gains from firm-level specialization based on technical excellence and economies of scale.[5] The sourcing by German motor vehicle manufacturers of air conditioning units from the French producer Valeo is an example of horizontal specialization. Specialization (whether vertical or horizontal) in turn involves linkages in the value chain that, again, entail movement in opposing directions.

Backward and forward linkages – Activity along the value chain involves both backward and forward linkages. Backward linkages, also referred to as demand-side effects, arise from imports used as inputs to GVC production. They are measured as the percentage of foreign value added in a country's exports. An example is the value added embodied in Chinese textiles used in Ethiopian clothing exports. Forward linkages, also referred to as supply-side effects, are measured as the percentage of a country's exported value added that is further exported by the importing country. An example of this is Kenyan cut-flower value added re-exported by Holland.

Trade in value added – The method of measuring trade in backward or forward linkages, known as trade in value added (TiVA), has the virtue of avoiding the double counting involved in conventional trade statistics when trade flows are measured gross and the values of products that cross borders several times for further processing are counted multiple times. The practical impact of TiVA measurement surfaced in the debate surrounding NAFTA reform when it was revealed that, within NAFTA value chains, the American share of value added in US imports from Mexico between 1995 and 2011 fell from 26 to 16 per cent while the Asian share rose from 7 to 20 per cent.[6]

The smile curve – The final dynamic involved in the economics of the GVC arises when measuring the value added at progressive stages of the chain. The result is commonly characterized as the smile curve, which, as one can imagine, shows that value added is highest in the early (product design) and late (product marketing) stages and lowest in the intermediate manufacturing stage.

One important implication of these complex interlinkages is that a shock within the supply chain can have a ripple effect much greater than that of the initial disruption.[7] Hence the link to concerns about vulnerability within the supply chain.

The fear of supply-chain vulnerability

As we have seen, well before the COVID-19 pandemic, global value chains were losing their force as drivers of world growth. Already during the cycle 2012–15, GVCs were playing a lesser stimulus role than they had done in the cycles of 1995–2000 and 2000–8. Concerns about the environmental footprint of globally fragmented production were a factor, as was automation, which reduced the labour intensity of manufacturing and the competitive advantage of low-wage countries, together with wages rising in those countries.

But rising protectionism was the principal reason for reduced GVC potency. This became even more apparent with the onset of punitive US action against China under the administration of Donald Trump. As one example, penalty tariffs against China led the Japanese firms Toshiba and Komatsu – at considerable cost – to shift the assembly part of their supply chain from China to Thailand and Mexico, but also, in a form of onshoring, to Japan itself.

COVID-19 – first identified from an outbreak in Wuhan, China, in December 2019 and declared a pandemic in March 2020 – transformed and accelerated these tendencies, as it triggered factory closures, transport restrictions and mounting national security concerns. The impact in some cases was transient – for example, the export restrictions impeding and distorting the supply chain for surgical facemasks. But elsewhere the effects have been far-reaching and persistent. Over 200 of Fortune Global 500 firms had a presence in Wuhan, and disruption to China-centred supply chains has seen plant closures affecting firms as diverse as Apple, Hyundai and Airbus. UNCTAD records global foreign direct investment – a key facilitator of globally fragmented production – falling by 30 to 40 per cent in 2020–1. World trade declined in nominal dollar terms by 9.6 per cent in 2020.

Now, added to COVID-19 disruption, we have – as anticipated in the previous chapter – the shocks imposed on the global value chain by the war in Ukraine and the related sanctions on and by Russia. The focus on this shock has, rightly, been directed at the food supply and energy chains. This was reflected in remarks by the German chancellor, Olaf Scholz, when he visited Canada in August 2022 to seal a green hydrogen purchase deal: 'Canada possesses as many raw materials as Russia but with the difference that it is a dependable democracy' (*Le Monde*, 18 September 2022). The global market for crucial metals is also an acute area of dependence and sensitivity concerning trade with Russia (see box 2).

And compounding all of these forces is the now intensified geopolitical rivalry between China and the United States and, to a somewhat lesser extent, between China and the European Union, Japan, South Korea, Australia and

Box 2 Global dependence on critical Russian raw materials

A number of countries – Türkiye (35 per cent of its imports are from Russia), Japan, Poland and China (each over 10 per cent) – are particularly dependent on Russia as a source of *aluminium* (a key material in vehicle and aircraft manufacture). Dependence on Russian *nickel* (used in transport and medical equipment, electronic devices and power generation) is also high for Finland (84 per cent of its imports), the Netherlands (34 per cent), Ukraine (23 per cent) and China (13 per cent). Russian *palladium* (used in catalytic converters and in capacitors that store energy in electronic devices) is of particular importance for Japan (43 per cent of its imports), the United States (37 per cent), the United Kingdom (30.5 per cent), China (28.5), Italy (26 per cent), Germany (21 per cent) and Korea (20 per cent).

Russian *vanadium oxides* (which improve the stability of steel alloys for space vehicles, nuclear reactors, aircraft and superconducting magnets) are of importance for the Czech Republic (88 per cent of imports), China (31 per cent) and India (21 per cent). Dependence on *potash* (a plant and crop nutrient) from Russia and Belarus is particularly high for Estonia (94.3 per cent of its imports), Nigeria (84 per cent), Türkiye (55.5 per cent), the European Union (51.5 per cent), Sri Lanka (50 per cent), Senegal (49 per cent), Brazil (27.4 per cent) and China (24.7 per cent).

Following Russia's invasion of Ukraine in February 2022 and, as of March 2022, suspension of cargo services to and from Russian ports by the major shipping companies, all of these metals showed considerably increased price peaks and volatility.

Data source: OECD (2023).

Canada. That rivalry, and its implications for global supply chains was vividly exposed in a speech given by the US treasury secretary Janet Yellen in Seoul in July 2022, when she said:

> We cannot allow countries, like China, to use their market position in key raw materials, technologies or products to have the power to disrupt our economy or exercise unwanted geopolitical leverage. Instead, the US and allies like South Korea should focus on friend-shoring or diversifying their supply chains to rely more on trusted trading partners, strengthening economic resilience and lowering risks.

But concern about supply-chain vulnerability is not exclusively a developed country phenomenon. Concerns about the dominance and practices of China within the global supply chain are also part of a shared ambivalence among the countries of Southeast Asia about the growing intensity of their economic links with Beijing.

And yet, as we saw in the introduction, concerns among both developed and developing countries about GVC vulnerability and the role of China are, somewhat paradoxically, accompanied by similar anti-globalization sentiment in China itself. Beijing's concerns arise, in large part, of course, from a fear of vulnerability to policy-driven constraints on the global trade on which the Chinese economy is now so dependent. This is leading to a departure from a growth model based on vast volumes of imported commodities and components and vast exports of manufactured products – a model known as *da jin da chu*, 'big in, big out'.

For developing countries more generally, the GVC indeed presents risks as well as benefits: a danger of becoming locked into low-value added parts of the chain; a risk of policy being determined by the priorities of the multinational enterprises that dominate the GVC; a risk of transmission through the GVC of macroeconomic and natural shocks, including increased sensitivity to individual elements of the business environment such as the costs of energy or specific regulations; and the danger that cooperation within a regional framework will simply entrench the distortions inherent in preferential trade arrangements. Some commentators have even argued that the emergence of value chains, and in particular the asymmetries in the governance structures that underpin them, pose a threat to sustainable economic development in the developing world.[8]

Against this, critics cannot deny that the most recent period of globalization and the development of the global value chain have seen a marked reduction in the income gap between North and South,[9] as developing countries, particularly in Asia, have become deeply engaged in the process of globally fragmented production.

The GVC offers three particular opportunities to developing countries: the possibility of specializing, according to their comparative advantage (again!), in one section of the value chain without having to master all stages; the possibility of reaping large economies of scale associated with global production; and the opportunity to associate fragmented production with the process of regional cooperation, often embodied in regional trade agreements.

Notwithstanding these benefits, developing as well as developed countries are using the trade weapon to reduce supply-chain dependence.

Moves to reduce dependence on the GVC are on two main tracks: first, the pursuit of increased national self-reliance via re-shoring of productive activity or de-linkage and, second, the redirection of trade towards regional and politically aligned partners via friend-shoring in what might be regarded as a form of increased *collective* self-reliance.

Let's look first at the de-linkage option and its shortcomings.

The pitfalls of de-linkage and re-shoring

A particularly aggressive use of the trade weapon is to promote selective supply-chain de-linkage by placing restraints on exports of essential and sensitive products or services, whether to favour domestic needs or to limit other countries' growth and, hence, future dependence on them. The standout case here is of course America's action against China.

American export controls on China: mainly self-harm

In October 2022, the Bureau of Industry and Security of the US Department of Commerce issued extensive new restrictions on exports to China of supercomputers, advanced semiconductors and related equipment – which it hoped would be as harmful to the Chinese economy generally as were previous US export controls on Huawei.[10] China itself has issued export controls on rare earths and crude oil and has been mulling an export ban on the silicon wafers used in solar panels.

US pressure mounted further in mid-December 2022, when the Commerce Department added thirty-six Chinese companies to its 'entity list', making it next to impossible to do business with them. A Bill was also introduced in the Senate to put Huawei and other Chinese companies on the US Treasury 'specially designated nationals' list that would deny them access to American banks, effectively excluding them from the global financial system.

US measures are designed to freeze China's semiconductor, or chip, technology at 2022 levels and impede its military development. This pressure will not end soon; both Republicans and Democrats see technological rivalry with China as an existential struggle. American tech-export controls on China will, however, wreak widespread damage, raising costs to consumers throughout the world, and without achieving their strategic objective. US restrictions will harm the United States itself by, perversely, accelerating the development of China's own chip-making capacity and by denying US firms the opportunities for growth through export; Intel, America's leading chip-maker, with sales of $21 billion to China in 2021, announced in October 2022 the axing of thousands of jobs.

The restrictions will also harm the regional supply chains of which China is an integral part, forcing countries such as Indonesia, Thailand and Vietnam to make the invidious choice between US- and China-centric tech supply chains. And because restrictions apply to any US technology, even non-American businesses whose products are derived from it are caught up.

America has persuaded Dutch and Japanese firms to adopt similar restrictive measures. And while the Taiwan Semiconductor Manufacturing Company and Korea's Samsung and SK Hynix were given a one-year waiver from the Bureau of Industry and Security regulations, a shadow was cast on the upgrading of their business in China. Meanwhile, in retaliation against the action on Huawei, Scandinavian vendors Ericsson and Nokia were squeezed out of China's 5G tenders.

Equally critically, US export controls will also harm the wider prospect of US–China cooperation in areas of mutual interest, such as the climate transition – as the world's two largest carbon emitters – debt relief – as the world's two largest aid donors – and reform and revival of the WTO.

Export controls are also subject to unintended consequences. Huawei – China's most successful network equipment vendor – has been the subject of the full weight of US export controls and denied access to vital components such as chipsets and virtualization software. But, as Hosuk Lee-Makiyama has pointed out, this is despite the fact that the quasi-private conglomerate has fewer ties with China's military or ruling party than outright state-owned companies such as ZTE. As a result, ZTE, despite its ties to the People's Liberation Army, continued to enjoy unfettered access to US technology, with corresponding benefits to its share price and bottom line.[11] According to the Rand Corporation, US tech restrictions will not significantly impede China's military development.

Given the shortcomings of *export* restrictions, the United States – and its allies – in seeking supply-chain de-linkage, will place equal, if not greater, emphasis on policies designed to boost national capacity – also referred to as re-shoring or re-localization. This track too is full of hazards.

Industry policy and the subsidy war: more self-harm

So-called industry policies, designed to foster targeted domestic sectors, have been identified in over a hundred countries, accounting for more than 90 per cent of global GDP (UNCTAD 2018). On occasion, it may make perfectly good sense for governments to target the development of national capacity. The announcement in September 2022 of the planned introduction of France's first offshore wind farms at Saint-Nazaire, in response to the energy crisis, could be a case in point. There is also evidence that advances in semiconductor technology are often boosted by government research grants (Miller 2022). And there may be a particular advantage, as appears to be the case in biotech drug production, in bringing manufacturing closer to its R&D (Pisano and Shih 2012).

But, as a general observation, the pursuit of industry policies triggers two warning lights. First, it is very difficult to target selected sectors (aerospace, medical devices, textiles, chemicals, active pharmaceutical ingredients, rare earths and semiconductors are frequently mentioned) without falling into the trap of 'picking winners'.[12] And, second – our main concern here – it is difficult to find industry-policy tools that don't involve protection and protectionist capture, leading to higher prices for consumers, reduced efficiency and, ultimately, reduced growth.

Among the tools being used increasingly to favour targeted domestic industries are preferences in public procurement. In the United States, for example, in the short period March to June 2022, US President Joe Biden invoked the Defense Production Act to encourage domestic production of no fewer than three favoured sectors: the extraction of minerals needed to make batteries for electric vehicles; the production of ingredients for infant formula; and the development of solar power.

But, today, the most widespread policy tool intended to reduce supply-chain dependence is the publicly funded subsidy. Indeed, one of the risks with the pursuit of the re-shoring of economic activity is of a trade-related subsidy war as countries seek to develop national capability – frequently under the cover of green innovation.

Starting with the more modest players, Japan has budgeted $2.3 billion to reconfigure supply chains, while India has allocated $26 billion in subsidies as 'production linked incentives' to fourteen industries in a bid to diversify away from China. The European Union, for its part, announced in February 2023 an initial outlay of €390 billion under its RepowerEU and InvestEU programmes, to be followed by further funding under a new EU budgetary instrument – all of this clearly intended to rival the subsidies being granted by the United States, with the attendant fear of tech poaching across the Atlantic. The fear may not be unfounded; during 2022, representatives of economic bodies from several US states, including Michigan and Ohio, toured Europe to tout the incentives being offered.[13]

But America is in a league of its own here. In its first two years, the Biden administration introduced subsidies valued at some $2 trillion in three salvos: the Infrastructure Act ($1.2 trillion), the CHIPS and Science Act ($280 billion) and the oddly named Inflation Reduction Act ($400 billion).

Semiconductors loom large in all of this, with America and the European Union allocating $76 billion and €11 billion, respectively, for chips development alone. China – not to be outdone — has itself spent some $80 billion on semiconductor subsidies, while massively increasing the role of the state via the state-owned enterprises. Moreover, in the case of semiconductors, the subsidy war risks accentuating the highly cyclical nature of the market for memory chips. Subsidies also are likely to endure; given the dispersed and esoteric physical inputs and intellectual property required, self-sufficiency in chips can take decades to acquire.

There is a particular irony in the use of subsidies in this way by the United States, the European Union and Japan, as these are precisely the countries constituting the 'Trilateral': a body calling explicitly for new disciplines within the WTO on subsidies they consider contribute to overcapacity. But beyond the irony there is a serious problem. A joint report recently prepared by the staff of the

International Monetary Fund, World Bank, WTO and OECD observes that the renewed drive towards industrial policies to promote 'strategic' sectors distorts international competition, especially against smaller, fiscally constrained developing countries, and that the increased frequency and complexity of distortive subsidies is bringing significant discord to the trading system (IMF et al. 2022).

And underlying this serious problem is a fundamental case of misdiagnosis. As Sébastien Miroudot (2020) has pointed out, in order to assess the severity of a supply-chain shock to growth, such as that flowing from the COVID-19 pandemic, it is necessary to compare falls in GDP and import intensity of production. There is no strong correlation. A country particularly dependent on the GVC, South Korea, had the lowest drop in GDP in 2020. In contrast, the EU, highly dependent on its regional supply chain but less on China, was severely hit by the COVID shock. The idea that dependence on China creates supply-chain vulnerability and that COVID has materialized this risk needs to be substantiated. COVID has clearly been highly disruptive, but the *scale* of disruption at the national level depends on many factors other than supply-chain links with China, and de-linkage from China would not, in this particular case, have been a decisive factor.

Equally fundamental, there is a strong body of evidence that the drop in GDP is higher under a re-localization scenario than with continued global links, because there are fewer channels for economic adjustment, higher costs, and higher volatility in output.[14] With re-shoring, firms also lose by being disconnected from the most efficient suppliers and from international knowledge networks. In addition, they may be exposed to greater cyber security risk if all firms use the same IT infrastructure. Moreover, Japanese experience suggests that subsidies to attract foreign companies to develop the country's domestic capacities, such as the $4.5 million subsidy to the Taiwanese semiconductor firm TSMC to set up in Japan, have tended to attract plants with low productivity, distant from the technological frontier.[15]

Another way of assessing the cost of re-localization is to consider the benefits forgone that come from curtailing the forward, and especially backward, linkages within the GVC that we examined at the beginning of this chapter. The supply-chain links between China and the countries of ASEAN are particularly instructive here.

China–ASEAN supply-chain links: a case study against decoupling

China's global value chain links with ASEAN are both less dominant and more beneficial than appears at first sight. With ASEAN public opinion seeking more alignment with the United States and less with China,[16] ASEAN's GVC dependence on the latter might be seen as cause for concern.

Over the past three decades, ASEAN trade links with the United States, the European Union and Japan have each weakened relative to those with China. Moreover, dependence on China has been more in backward linkages (where China's share of foreign value-added exports incorporated in ASEAN exports has risen from 5 to 17 per cent) than in forward links (where China's share of ASEAN value-added exports incorporated in other countries' exports has risen from 4 to just 12 per cent).

But this account needs nuance. ASEAN links with the US, the EU and Japan are not weakened as much as it appears. And the links with China are highly beneficial to ASEAN. The relatively weaker trade links between ASEAN and the US, the EU and Japan have been largely compensated by increased market-seeking and efficiency-seeking investment and production, within ASEAN, of affiliates of these countries.[17] ASEAN's GVC links beyond China have been transformed rather than weakened. It is precisely the presence of these globally oriented, transnational affiliates that helps explain ASEAN's strong, and otherwise surprising, forward linkages with, in particular, the European Union.

Indeed, when account is taken of intra-EU trade – Europe's regional value chain – the EU accounts for a greater (albeit declining) share of ASEAN exports incorporated into other countries' exports (28 per cent) than does China (12 per cent), as seen in table 2. ASEAN, through its forward linkages, is more integrated with the EU GVC than with that of China – particularly in technologically advanced sectors such as electronics.

But the most important corrective to an alarmist narrative of ASEAN GVC bonds with China is that backward links with China are fostering development within ASEAN. It is in fact the paucity of these backward linkages, and correspondingly limited access to foreign value added, for ASEAN small and medium-sized enterprises (SMEs) that help explain why SMEs play a disproportionately minor role in ASEAN exports. ASEAN SMEs have had less exposure to 'learning by importing'.[18]

Backward links are, however, not equally shared throughout ASEAN. While Malaysia, Singapore, Thailand and Vietnam are developing a manufacturing base with strong backward links (foreign value added makes up 60 per cent of ASEAN vehicle exports), Brunei, Indonesia, Laos and Myanmar remain dependent on natural resource activities with weak backward links (foreign value added makes up just 5 per cent of Indonesia's agribusiness exports). This means that policy settings will need to differ by country. Nevertheless, all ASEAN states – and indeed developing countries more generally – will in future face three common GVC challenges: an increase in the importance of inward

Table 2: ASEAN's value-added exports incorporated into other countries' exports (forward links)

	1990		2018	
	$m	%	$m	%
World	25,565		372,286	
European Union	7,769	30.4	102,843	27.6
United States	935	3.7	11,094	3.0
Japan	3,010	11.8	31,271	8.4
China	897	3.5	43,671	11.7
Korea	1,264	4.9	28,620	7.7
ASEAN	5,173	20.0	114,655	30.8

Source: Data from ASEAN-Japan Centre, *Global value chains in ASEAN*, January 2019.

investment relative to trade; more focus on domestic demand in dynamic partner economies; and the persistence of GVC vulnerability to disruption. China will be central to all these challenges.

It may be expected that, as China moves to counter its demographic aging and rising domestic costs, it will increasingly follow the path already taken by the US, the EU and Japan in favouring investment over trade in its GVC links with ASEAN. Already, China's foreign direct investment (FDI) in Southeast Asia grew fourfold between 2010 and 2018. Given the sovereignty concerns associated with inward FDI, this shift will need to involve a change in China's 'tendency to downplay the autonomous agency' of developing neighbours.[19] Equally critical, however, will be ASEAN's own policy settings to maximize gain from investment inflows, including through stronger environmental safeguards, technological upgrading and greater domestic regulatory coherence.

ASEAN's second GVC challenge will be a shift in the relative importance of final consumption (rather than onward export) within partner economies with expanding domestic markets. This again will call for adaptability in ASEAN as it shifts product design towards, in particular, China's domestic consumers as opposed to China's overseas customers – consistent with China's domestically oriented Dual Circulation Strategy.

The third GVC challenge facing ASEAN is persistent vulnerability to disruption. This will call for flexibility and resilience, whether by removing hand-picked fibres from the textiles supply chain to deal with Uyghur labour concerns or by strengthening digital supply networks, fostering the automation of traditional manufacturing (Industry 4.0) and backing international efforts to promote a liberal, 'technoglobalist' view of the open internet that seeks to engage rather than isolate Beijing.

Despite these formidable GVC challenges, what ASEAN should not do is to seek to decouple from the supply chain. OECD modelling suggests that such decoupling, by reducing exposure to upstream supply shocks, would slightly improve

ASEAN's economic stability (by one-fifth of a percentage point of GDP) but massively reduce growth (by over 10 per cent of GDP) (OECD 2021a). Growth loss occurs precisely because of reduced backward linkages – the same backward linkages that also help explain why only Asian countries have been catching up with the rich world.[20]

Another thing that ASEAN, and developing countries generally, should not do is to dust off old infant industry policies. It might be suggested that the advent of the GVC has strengthened the case for infant industry protection[21] by enhancing the possibilities for learning by doing. The new trade theory could even be invoked in support of this proposition, given its focus on increasing returns to scale.

In other ways, however, the fragmentation inherent in the GVC – and the complex interaction of trade, investment and technology – has exposed the weaknesses of the infant industry argument: by making it even harder for government to pick winners with the potential to become internationally competitive; by reducing the scope to develop a whole national supply chain in a trade environment built on the performance of tasks; by constraining the ability of governments to adopt industry-specific policy in the face of business strategies increasingly governed by multinational company priorities; and by placing a premium on reducing rather than increasing barriers to trade.[22]

It has indeed been suggested (Baldwin 2012) that a reason developing countries abandoned pro-industrialization policies from the pre-ICT era – including import substitution and local content restrictions – was that they were hindrances to joining global supply chains.

Once within the GVC, the risk of continuing to pursue protectionist policies – with the attendant risk of protectionist capture – is of increasing the dispersion of tariffs (the most serious element of distortion) as barriers are lowered on intermediate inputs but maintained, or increased, on final products and services.

In summing up this discussion of the hazards of re-shoring and de-linkage, let's consider the broad implications for the process of globalization.

Re-shoring: not the end of globalization, but still a matter for concern

We need to be clear that the pursuit of re-shoring, when invoked as a trade weapon in the search for self-reliance, does not spell the end of globalization. Self-reliance has its limits: it will always be a relative and selective thing. Even vast economies such as those of the United States and China depend on trade; total self-sufficiency is not a realistic objective. Indeed, the goal of Washington, Beijing and Brussels is not autarky but, rather, to the contrary, a dominant presence within the global value chain, together with greater self-reliance in designated sensitive areas.

Going back to basics, David Ricardo's foundational insight (yes, him again!) that a country will export the product in which, on the basis of domestic opportunity cost, it has a comparative advantage and import the product in which it has a comparative disadvantage has proved remarkably robust. As the former UK Treasury minister Jim O'Neill has put it, so long as firms seek to satisfy customers with the highest quality products at the lowest possible prices, globalization will remain a fact of economic life.[23]

The central place of China within the GVC will also remain a fact of economic life, with its vast domestic market and workforce, deep supplier networks and reliable infrastructure. The case of the German firm BASF, the world's largest chemicals company, is highly instructive in this respect. BASF, aiming to achieve net-zero carbon-dioxide emissions by 2050, is investing $10 billion in a state-of-the-art site in Zhanjiang in southern China. The rationale for this development is the expectation that China, which already represents about half the world market for chemicals, will account for more than three-quarters of that market's global growth in the next few years.[24]

The data reflect the continuing importance of global trade ties. After dipping in 2020, the share of trade in global GDP bounced back sharply in 2021, and this is not counting the growth of traded digital services and ideas, not always captured in trade statistics.[25] Admittedly, the United

States and China are seeking to decouple sensitive parts of their economies from each other, including in dual-use technology where innovations can be used for aggressive as well as peaceful ends. But comparisons with Cold War rivalry with the Soviet Union are misleading. The Chinese Communist Party bears little resemblance to its Soviet predecessor. Its 'socialism with Chinese characteristics' aims to mobilize capitalism's strength as a means of resource allocation, not to overthrow it. And the party aims not to employ Chinese socialism as an instrument of geopolitical subversion but to contain organized political activity at home (Gupta 2022).

The US–China relationship is thus likely to evolve into what the former Australian prime minister Kevin Rudd calls 'managed strategic competition'.[26] In fact, trade between the US and China continues to increase – bilateral goods trade growing 19 per cent in 2021 and reaching a record high of $690.6 billion in 2022. Japan's links with China show a similar degree of ambivalence. While outlaying subsidies of $2.3 billion in 2020 to promote the re-shoring of production (in what in the Japanese press were called China exit subsidies), Japan, in the same year, directed $12 billion in FDI into China, aimed at higher value-added business.

And although stated intentions to re-shore are widespread, the actual amount of re-localization is probably, so far, relatively modest. A study by Lucy Eldridge and Susan Powers (2018) of the US Bureau of Labor Statistics is particularly useful in showing that, over the past two decades, imports into the United States have actually grown (from 8 to 10 per cent) as a share of all intermediate inputs – materials, services and energy – used by US firms to produce goods and services. A key determinant of how much re-localization is likely to happen is the extent to which the trading majors face actual supply-chain vulnerability. Again, this is less than one might expect. A review by the European Commission identified 137 of 5,000 imported products with a dominant foreign supplier. Of those, only some thirty-four were hard to substitute by using other suppliers, representing just 0.6 per cent of EU imports by value.

But all this said, decoupling sentiment is widespread. Massive distorting subsidies are being expended. And protectionist capture – combined with persisting geopolitical tension – risks entrenching those distortions and further strengthening the headwinds that the GVC has been facing over the past ten years. This prompts the question: Is there a more effective way than subsidy-fuelled re-shoring and de-linkage to address concerns about supply-chain vulnerability? Fortunately, the answer is 'yes'.

A better way: some implications for policy makers

There would seem to be general agreement that the principal requirement in reducing the risk of supply-chain shocks is to improve resilience (to de-risk). There is disagreement, however, about how such resilience is best achieved and, indeed, about what resilience even means.

First, the definitional question. In risk management literature, resilience is defined as 'the ability of a system to return to its original state or move to a more desirable state after being disturbed' (Christopher and Peck 2004). So resilience is about reducing the time it takes for companies to resume normal production once a disruption has occurred. It is different from robustness, which is the ability of the supply chain to maintain its functioning despite internal or external disruption. Calls for more resilience are often confused with the pursuit of robustness (Miroudot 2020). As to how resilience might be achieved (short of outright de-linkage), some of the advocated approaches are clearly more effective than others.

Diversification, regionalization and the pursuit of friend-shoring: a hazardous second track?

Much vaunted is the principle of supplier diversification within the supply chain. In the literature, this is also referred to as 'redundancy' (diversifying suppliers so that one or more can be dispensed with, or made redundant, should the need arise). Diversification is very much a case-by-case matter. It needs to be determined whether the cost of diversifying to new suppliers will be less than the cost of disruption with the current supplier, depending on the availability, reliability and price of alternative supplies, the level of stocks held by the buyer, and the anticipated length and severity of the disruption. Some situations will be relatively clear-cut. Countries such as Germany, Estonia or Finland that in 2022 were highly dependent on Russian gas (with hindsight, perhaps too asymmetrically dependent, given Russia's actions in Crimea in 2014) had little choice but to diversify away from Moscow. There is also empirical evidence showing that firms with more diversified suppliers are more resilient in times of epidemic.[27]

Driven in part by concerns at China's trade obstructionism and economic espionage, Japan's Economic Security Bill, which passed in the Diet in May 2022, is strongly focused on supply-chain diversification. And in a survey conducted in 2020, the consulting firm McKinsey found that over 80 per cent of supply-chain leaders are sourcing raw materials from two suppliers rather than one. Even in clear-cut cases, however, diversification needs to be accompanied by other practices, notably in inventory management and sharing, to reduce future vulnerability. We will come back to this later.

In other situations, the case for diversification may be much less clear. A study based on the examination of 4,000 US firms finds that supply chains with more diversified sourcing have slower recovery after disruption than chains relying on single sourcing. This happens because single sourcing is associated with long-term relationships that ensure faster recovery, as suppliers are more committed to mitigating risk. Multiple sourcing also means greater cost through having to maintain larger inventories (Jain et al. 2016).

As to friend-shoring, while on occasion this too may make good sense (as for example with German purchases of Canadian green hydrogen), if trade is not already occurring with 'friends', this may well be because it doesn't make commercial sense. Moreover, who is a 'friend'? It has been suggested, for example, that EU dependence on US gas makes it vulnerable to American pressure to transfer personal digital data.²⁸ And how do you stop firms from buying from the cheapest source? The ultimate logic of friend-shoring would be to split the world into rival trade blocs. Recent research at the IMF and WTO highlights the costs of such a split, entailing serious financial fragmentation, particularly damaging for developing countries, and major losses in GDP, as high as 12 per cent in some regions.²⁹

And as for regionalization, the same question arises as with friend-shoring: if regional links have not already been established, it suggests that they may not be optimal. And if they are viable only on the basis of regional preferences then, again, this may be a second-best approach. This said, there may be scope for flexibility, at the regional level, in the location of business activity. For example, in the early stage of the COVID-19 pandemic, Samsung temporarily moved its mobile phone production from Korea to Vietnam when its factory was threatened by the pandemic.

The 2020 World Investment Report of UNCTAD was already predicting that diversification and regionalization – as well as re-shoring – will drive the restructuring of GVCs in coming years. This is by no means sure. It does not conform with the main body of GVC analysis. And, more importantly, it is not grounded in actual business experience.

Pointers on the right path to resilience: the domestic policy focus

A first step in designing policies to promote resilience in supply chains is perhaps to recognize that a global shock does not mean that supply chains in all sectors will be affected identically. Recovery rates from the 2008–9 global financial crisis suggest that supply chains in mining and quarrying are much less prone to external shocks than are those in, say, motor vehicle production. This is because they have a relatively higher services component, typically less prone to cyclical movements than manufacturing, and a less diversified bundle of technologically complex products (Jouanjean et al. 2017). Policies need to adapt accordingly.

A common sector-wide requirement, however, is the development of efficiency-enhancing digital supply networks based on functional silos but linked by the use of big data analytics and the Internet of Things (Birkel and Hartman 2020). Such approaches can be used in identifying threats to essential activities, prioritizing shipments of essential goods and services, seeking upstream agreements with firms for the repurposing of supply chains, and calibrating stockpiles of essential goods to reduce the need for emergency refills. For example, during the early outbreak of COVID-19, 3M, one of the biggest producers of facemasks, announced that it would spend $500 million on the digital network in order to reduce the cost of stock holding.

What the use of digitalization in this way means is that, contrary to the claim often made, it is not necessary to replace 'just in time' inventory management for a costlier, more precautionary 'just in case' approach. Efficiency does not need to be sacrificed in the pursuit of resilience. The success of digitalization will depend critically on action taken at the level of the firm. This is not to say, however, that there is no role for government. Scope exists, for example, for public–private partnerships in stockpiling and for the establishment of national stockpiles beyond the capacity of firms to ramp up production.

Government has an important role to play too in improving the regulation of transport and infrastructure, organizing and monitoring stress tests for GVC viability, streamlining border procedures, including potentially for 'processing trade',[30] and establishing public–private platforms at the level of the GVC (Hoekman 2014). Intergovernmental cooperation can also play an important role. Based on OECD work on the security of supply for critical raw materials, the G7 has committed to ongoing strategic coordination to identify, monitor and minimize vulnerabilities and logistical bottlenecks in the face of external shocks and wider risks (OECD 2022). The discussion in the previous chapter of responses to specific sanctions-related concerns in Europe about energy supply is largely a matter of intergovernmental cooperation.

Government also has an essential – and not always acknowledged – role in shaping the overall national policy framework within which firms conduct their supply-chain activities. For all countries, domestic reform can spur resilience and recovery prospects. For example, lowering restrictions on service imports can increase the quality of service inputs and the exports of service-intensive manufactures. More effective competition policies can spur innovation, ultimately leading to more export diversification. A useful way of illustrating the role of the domestic policy framework is in the context of the Supply Chain Resilience Initiative being pursued by the governments of India, Japan and Australia (see box 3).

> **Box 3 The Supply Chain Resilience Initiative: it's the domestic economy, stupid**
>
> Currently under way is a trilateral exploration by Japan, India and Australia of a Supply Chain Resilience Initiative (SCRI) seeking to secure supply chains and reduce dependence on China. The initiative, instigated by Japan, is envisaged to extend eventually to ASEAN and the United States.
>
> An immediate question arising is what degree of shared strategic ambition exists among this rather disparate group of countries. India and Japan have clear economic motivations – including fostering Indian pharmaceutical activity in Japan and Australia and Japanese motor vehicle production in India. But distinctive strategic concerns also arise from ongoing border tensions with China in East Ladakh and the Senkaku islands.
>
> The driving ambition of the United States is no less than to constrain China's rising technological and strategic prowess. But although Australia may wish to have fewer eggs in the China basket, it will not want to jeopardize crucial trade links with the region's largest market. And ASEAN members, whose participation is unlikely, are ambivalent decouplers.

Moreover, is there a realistic alternative to China? India and the US might by virtue of their size be considered possible alternatives within certain supply chains – yet both have policy settings that act against this. India consistently fails to capitalize on its comparative advantage in manufacturing, and the United States imposes self-harming restrictions on the spread of its technology.

This is not to say that there is no role for the SCRI. But the focus will need to be less on sectoral reconfiguration and picking winners and more on cooperative efforts to improve overall supply-chain functioning. This calls for better harnessing of technology in supply-chain management, freer cross-border data flows, and greater regulatory coherence in digital trade protocols. But the overriding requirement in improving supply-chain resilience and effectiveness is better domestic economic policies within the countries engaged in them – that is, policies that strengthen both backward and forward linkages.

For prospective SCRI participants, such policies will be country specific. India must develop simpler labour laws, improve basic infrastructure, and promote openness in the digital economy. Japan should foster improvements in productivity via enhanced corporate governance to offset the impact of falling labour inputs. The United States would do well to return to more open policies of technological development, enabling it to 'run faster'. And Australia, in line with its Department of Foreign Affairs and Trade's COVID-19 parliamentary enquiry submission, should avoid 'rigid production systems based on the worst and most infrequent of events'.

In brief, if the SCRI is not to be a slippery slope, it will need to focus less on decoupling from China and more on domestic and cooperative action to improve the enabling environment in which supply chains operate.

In formulating government policy to improve supply-chain functioning, in the presence of growing geopolitical tensions, a tricky question arising is whether it is possible to engage with repressive autocracies without seeming to condone their behaviour.

Engaging with autocracies within the global value chain: 'trading with the enemy'?

The practical question of engagement with autocracies arises most frequently in connection with China.

In the wake of the global financial crisis, China began to move away from the market-based approach that had shaped its economic policies for three decades. Moreover, under Xi Jinping, China's world view has become increasingly combative, grounded on the assumption of 'external attempts to blackmail, contain, blockade and exert maximum pressure on China'.[31] It is also the case that China, along with Russia, is commonly seen as leading an essentially Eurasian grouping of dangerous states, including the likes of Iran, North Korea and Pakistan. And, consistent with its world view, China is increasingly seen to bully and harass smaller states that cross its path.

Yet, there is also a point of view – shared here – that Western nations' relations with China need to be differentiated and conducted according to the field of interest. There will inevitably be areas of confrontation, as with China's military adventurism in the South China Sea. There will, equally, be areas of cooperation, as with international efforts to manage the climate transition. And, between these two, there will be areas of competition, as in the conduct of trade and commercial relations. In the words of the Australian prime minister Anthony Albanese, 'co-operate where we can, disagree where we must and engage in our national interest.'

Two qualifications need to be made to this characterization of relations with China. The first is that the weight placed on the three elements of confrontation, cooperation and competition will vary among Western nations, depending on their respective size and geostrategic importance. Notions of strategic rivalry with China will loom larger for a major power such as the United States than for a small or medium sized player.³² The second qualification is that acknowledgement of the competitive aspect of trade should not be allowed to obscure the underlying common interest among trading partners, including, as we saw in the discussion of ASEAN supply-chain links with China, the gains that come from importing.

The question may nevertheless arise: is there not a risk of political contagion when doing business with autocracies? The academic literature is somewhat divided – as it often is – on how trade with autocracies influences political outlook. In one recent study, Benny Kleinman, Ernest Liu and Stephen Redding of Princeton University found that, over the period 1980 to 2010, the more economically connected a country became with China, the more political alignment ensued, as seen in patterns of UN voting and the forming of alliances (Kleinman et al. 2020). Another paper, however, by Giacomo Magistretti of the IMF and Marco Tabellini of Harvard University, finds, more reassuringly, that, while a rise in trade links with democratic countries raises a country's Polity score (measuring the democracy rating of a country's governing institutions) quite markedly, trade with autocracies has no such (contrary) effect (Magistretti and Tabellini 2022).³³

Whatever the relationship between trade links and political outlook, the important requirement is that, from a trade policy perspective – and in the interest of discouraging use of the trade weapon within the GVC – trade relations with autocracies be conducted within the framework of disciplines embodied in the WTO or regional groupings, such as the Regional Comprehensive Economic Partnership (RCEP), of which China is a member. This engagement via the WTO is made all the more important given that private companies, such as BASF, will continue to foster their supply-chain relationship with China on the basis of purely commercial considerations;³⁴ it is better that that relationship is played out under commonly agreed rules – rules with which, as we will see in the next chapter, China is in part, but by no means comprehensively, compliant.

Earlier hopes that trade and financial engagement with Beijing – including via WTO membership – would prompt a sustained market-oriented economic and social transformation in China have proved unrealistic, perhaps naïve. Moreover, Immanuel Kant has unfortunately been proved wrong in saying that 'the spirit of trade cannot co-exist with war.' None of this, however, provides an argument for disengagement.

Closing thoughts

Our discussion of ways of avoiding use of the trade weapon to dismantle or weaken global supply chains prompts a few observations.[35]

Although the combined effects of COVID-19 disruption, the Ukraine war and rising geopolitical friction are unprecedented, earlier major catastrophes such as the terrorist attacks of 2001, Hurricane Katrina in 2005, the Tōhoku earthquake and tsunami in Japan, and the Chao Phraya floods in Thailand in 2011 have demonstrated that companies can respond to such shocks, and bounce back, by reinforcing their risk-management strategies, without resorting to re-shoring or friend-shoring. GVCs are more resilient than one might think. While intermediate trade fell by 10 per cent in the first half of 2020, by the third quarter it had reached pre-pandemic levels (WTO 2022).

Indeed, there is no reason to believe that using the trade weapon (notably the state subsidy) to reduce interdependence in pursuit of self-reliance would reduce exposure to economic risk. Moreover, there is a serious danger of confusing the case for GVC resilience with arguments for bringing jobs back home – fuelling protectionist tendencies and the risk of protectionist capture. It will not help to seek to replace GVC links with domestic production where that production can only survive behind a protective wall.

The key to a country getting the full benefits out of the GVC is to have a sound, overall domestic policy framework. And, while there is a role for government in supply-chain management, this does not mean the need for a new paradigm for the GVC. Where supply-chain concerns are accompanied by worries about rule-breaking abuses by trading partners within the chain – notably China – the answer is neither the pursuit of self-sufficiency nor a resort to unilateral self-defence and the risk of further weakening the already enfeebled WTO. The answer, rather, is to use the WTO to address those abuses. This is the subject of our next chapter.

3
Trade Self-Defence

Countries are concerned about vulnerability and dependence in trade, regardless of whether their trading partners play by the rules – the subject of the previous chapter. When trading partners do not play by the rules, or are considered not to do so, then an additional concern arises. Unfortunately, the pursuit of self-reliance in response to the first concern (vulnerability) weakens the authority of the rules-based system needed to address the second concern (rule-breaking). This in turn leads to power-based unilateral approaches to trade defence in the name of national sovereignty[1] and, on occasion, national security.

There has always been a tension in the WTO between the exercise of sovereignty by independent nation-states, who make up the membership, and respect for the rules-based system in defence of the liberal trading order.[2] As part of the backlash against globalization, the pursuit of national sovereignty is in the ascendency in that tussle.

This chapter looks at how the enfeebling of the WTO, and particularly its dispute settlement mechanism, is fuelling unilateralism in the use of the trade weapon in self-defence against alleged unfair trade practices or to provide a form of safety valve. Though undertaken in the name of national sovereignty, such usage imposes major costs on the users while provoking trade friction and further weakening the rules-based trading order.

But, first, we need to look in a little more detail at the nature of trade defence.

Trade remedies: a dominant and protectionist force

Trade remedies (also called commercial instruments, trade defence measures or, often by economists, contingent protection) are used in two general situations: to face allegedly unfair trade practices in the form of dumping of products on a market or the use of subsidies and to provide some form of 'safety valve' in the form of safeguard actions to deal with unforeseen import surges.[3] Importantly, there are WTO provisions that provide for the use of each of these measures: GATT Article VI in the case of anti-dumping duties and countervailing duties to offset the effects of a trading partner's export subsidies and Article XIX in the case of safeguard measures when an unforeseen surge in imports causes or threatens serious injury. Overall, trade remedies are by far the most common trade measure – representing 41 per cent of all non-COVID-related trade restrictions implemented by the G20 economies in the period May 2022 to October 2022 (WTO 2022). And, within trade remedies, by far the most common tool is anti-dumping action.[4] We will therefore concentrate on that.

Dumping is said to occur when the price of the good in the importing country is below the price of that good in the exporting country's home market. The critical question then arising is whether the flexibility granted by the use of trade remedies allows countries to make greater liberalization commitments because of the reassurance given of temporary relief from increased import competition or whether such contingency measures are used as a tool of protection, with the attendant risk of protectionist capture.

A first warning indicator of the protection scenario is the fact that anti-dumping initiations are strongly counter-cyclical, rising during slowdowns in global activity, suggesting an opportunistic pattern as anti-dumping action is taken against producers in multiple jurisdictions rather than as a case-by-case response to trade abuse by specific commercial partners (see figure 1).[5] Although the pattern observed could partly reflect the fact that injury from dumping is likely to be more acutely felt during downswings in economic activity, a close examination of the practice of anti-dumping action confirms the protectionist interpretation.

An inquiry conducted in Australia highlights a plethora of practices that increase the protectiveness of the anti-dumping system and the scope for abuse of this practice (Productivity Commission 2016). For example, the scope to use proxy or constructed normal values in dumping cases has been widened. Typically, these methodologies will be more likely to lead to a finding of dumping than the previous default methodology based on prices in the exporter's home market. In addition, the Anti-Dumping Commission has, for the first time, employed 'zeroing' in calculating a dumping margin. The practice, which has attracted adverse findings from the WTO Dispute Resolution Body, involves attaching a zero

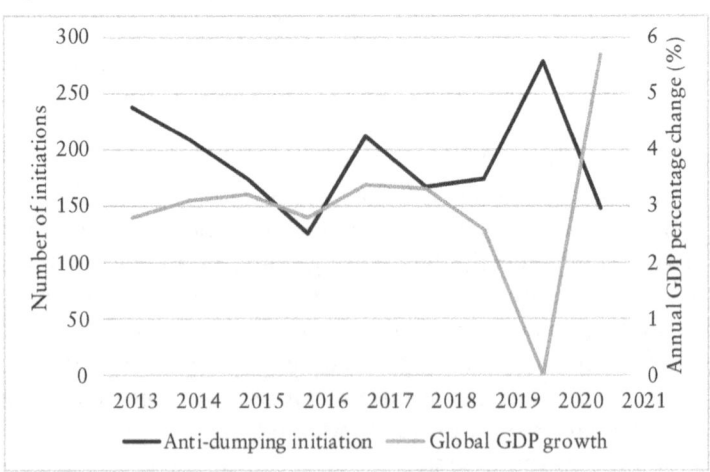

Figure 1: Anti-dumping and the business cycle

Source: Data from World Bank national accounts and WTO anti-dumping initiations.

weight to any sales of un-dumped goods within an overall bundle of sales that is examined to determine whether dumping has occurred. Zeroing increases the likelihood of finding that there has been dumping, the estimated average dumping margin and the size of the duty subsequently imposed.

A practical indication of the protective nature of Australia's anti-dumping regime comes from a case in which Indonesia took Australia to the WTO over its imposition of anti-dumping duties on A4 copy paper. Australia lost the case in late 2019.

The global targets of anti-dumping actions also tend to support the protectionist interpretation of their use. Within the sectoral pattern of AD action there is a dominance of the metals, metal products and chemical industries – sectors strongly susceptible to trade and politically sensitive because of their high labour intensity.

Between 2008 and 2021, 28 per cent of anti-dumping initiations were directed at China. The second most targeted country was the Republic of Korea, accounting for just 6 per cent of all initiations (WTO 2022). The focus on China is consistent with the protection-based interpretation of anti-dumping action and the fact that the designation of China as a non-market economy by the United States and the European Union is driven largely by the political economy of trade remedies. This is worth looking at in a little more detail.

Anti-dumping and the special case of China

A crucial question in the application of anti-dumping action is the way in which the dumping margin is determined. This has particular resonance in the case of countries considered to be 'non-market economies'. In such cases, anti-dumping investigators can use proxies to estimate the home market prices or costs of the foreign exports in determining whether dumping takes place. Such proxies, however, are defined in such a way that they make it easier to prove dumping than in the case of market economies. And they inflate the dumping margin.[6]

This issue has particular relevance for China because it is the principal global target for anti-dumping action and because it is not recognized as a market economy by either the United States or the European Union (nor indeed by Australia). In the framework of the WTO, the determination of China's status – whether market economy or non-market economy – hinges on the interpretation of the terms of its accession to the organization in December 2001. This has been the subject of some insightful analysis by Laura Puccio of the EU Commission Legal Service.[7] China's interpretation of the accession protocol is that its trading partners could consider it to be a non-market economy only until the end of 2016, at which time it would be recognized as a market economy. The US and EU interpretation is that, at the end of 2016, China's status would be reviewed.

The two key elements of the accession protocol are contained in the following extracts.

Section 15(a)(ii)
The importing WTO Member may use a methodology that is not based on a strict comparison with domestic prices or costs in China if the producers under investigation cannot clearly show that market economy conditions prevail in the industry producing the like product with regard to manufacture, production and sale of that product.

Section 15(d)
In any event, the provisions of subparagraph 15(a)(ii) shall expire 15 years after the date of accession. In addition, should China establish, pursuant to the national law of the importing WTO Member, that market economy conditions prevail in a particular industry or sector, the non-market economy provisions of subparagraph (a) shall no longer apply to that industry or sector.

It is the ambiguity within Section 15(d) of the accession protocol that allows China to argue, from the first sentence, that the 2016 expiry of section 15(a)(ii) entails the automatic granting of market-economy status to China and the EU and US to argue, from the second sentence, that it does not. This matter does not seem set for early resolution. In the case of the EU, a non-market economy applying for economy-wide market-economy status in the framework of anti-dumping investigations must prove that it meets five criteria:

1 a low degree of government influence in the allocation of resources and in decisions of enterprises;
2 an absence of distortion in the operation of the privatized economy;
3 the effective implementation of company law with adequate corporate governance rules;
4 an effective legal framework for the conduct of business and proper functioning of a free-market economy (including intellectual property rights and bankruptcy laws);
5 the existence of a genuine financial sector.

In the United States, determination of market-economy status is based on six factors:

1 the presence of currency manipulation;
2 the determination of wages following free labour market dynamics;
3 openness to joint ventures and foreign investment;
4 the extent of government ownership and control of production means;
5 the extent of government control over the allocation of resources (pricing and output decisions);
6 any other relevant factor.

The tone of the 2021 Annual Report to Congress of the US–China Economic and Security Review Commission suggests that China's non-market economy status is unlikely to change soon. The report, while noting 'a decade long slowdown trend' and a '14th Five Year Plan that acknowledges underlying structural problems', asserts that 'China's leaders believe they can address these challenges through more state-led technology development and by strengthening rather than loosening the government's control over the economy' (US–China Economic and Security Review Commission 2021).

Before concluding this discussion of the protective nature of trade remedy action, it is worth noting a particular feature of such action that greatly increases its potency. As we saw in the introduction, the threat of action alone can be sufficient to cause significant trade and investment distortion without any penalties actually being imposed.

As with all cases of petitions for protection – 60 per cent of which are successful in America – it is the customer who pays. A study of safeguard tariffs granted to the US washing-machine maker Whirlpool is instructive. In 2017, the United States International Trade Commission instigated tariffs of 20 per cent, rising to 50 per cent above a quota of 1.2 million units in the first year. The result, according to a study by Aaron Flaaen and his colleagues at the Federal Reserve, was an increase in the retail price of washing machines in the United States of 12 per cent (Flaaen et al. 2020).

It should be stressed that all the trade remedy measures described so far, their shortcomings notwithstanding, have been undertaken within the framework of the WTO. They do not, as considered here, strictly constitute the weaponization of trade. They do, however, show the potential for trade defence to be a protectionist tool. That feature is now compounded by two growing tendencies, both of which constitute weaponization.

The first situation arises when countries, opportunistically, invoke the WTO trade defence provisions in the service of other goals. A case in point is the penalty tariff imposed by China in 2020 against the import of Australian barley and wine, at respectively 80 and 212 per cent, for alleged dumping but in fact, as widely perceived, as punishment for Canberra's call for an independent inquiry into the origins of the COVID-19 virus. At least here, though the damage was already done, Australia could use the framework of GATT Article VI to take China to dispute settlement. This is not so easy with the second development: the disturbing tendency among the trading majors to pursue trade remedies on a unilateral basis outside, or in breach of, the disciplines – albeit imperfect – of the WTO. We turn to that now.

Growing unilateral, power-based use of the trade weapon: in the name of sovereignty and national security

The United States

In 2018, under the presidency of Donald Trump, the United States unleashed three salvos of the trade weapon, instigated unilaterally under US domestic law, drawing respectively on:

- Section 232 of the US Trade Expansion Act of 1962: tariffs on steel and aluminium, at respectively 25 per cent and 10 per cent, plus threatened tariffs on motor vehicle imports, invoked to counter threats to US national security,
- Section 201 of the US Trade Act of 1974: tariffs on solar cells, invoking unfair trade practices, and
- Section 301 of the 1974 Trade Act: penalty tariffs of between 10 and 25 per cent on $250 billion, and potentially more, of imports from China, including aerospace, ICT and machinery invoked to counter Chinese intellectual property right (IPR) breaches.

In each of these cases, America imposed tariffs above the bound rates to which it had committed under WTO rules and without resorting to WTO disciplines such as the Safeguards Agreement, specifically designed to deal with unforeseen import surges or perceived breaches of WTO rules and with vital links to the principles of non-discrimination, coherence and proportionality. The United States did in part, however, invoke GATT Article XXI which, as we saw in the introduction, allows members to violate WTO rules where it considers essential security interests to be at risk. This is a disputed area of WTO jurisprudence that is worth exploring a little more.

GATT Article XXI allows a member state to violate WTO rules when it considers it 'necessary for the protection of its essential security interests'. This right is not questioned; what is questioned is whether the security exception can be unilaterally invoked – as the US believes – or whether it should be authorized by an external body. This matter came to a head in 2018, when the United States sought to justify its steel and aluminium tariffs under Article XXI – arguing that such action precluded WTO Dispute Settlement Panels from examining counter-claims by targeted countries.

The matter was resolved – in a fashion – in 2019 under the Russia – Traffic in Transit Dispute Settlement Panel, which found that dispute settlement judges can evaluate whether an invocation of Article XXI is justified. But, once this evaluation is made, a member can still pursue the action that it considers necessary, regardless of the panel's judgement, in a legitimate exercise of its Article XXI rights. This will now be put to the test, as in December 2022 WTO dispute settlement panels ruled that the Trump administration's invocation of Article XXI when imposing penalty tariffs on steel and aluminium was not justified. Respected trade lawyers Petros Mavroidis and Sunayana Sasmal of Columbia University have expressed the view that the 2019 panel approach achieves the right balance of managing competing interests in multilateralism, abusive constructs of protectionism and legitimate assertions of sovereignty (Sasmal and Mavroidis 2022).

It is indeed a finely balanced judgement but one that, nevertheless, fails to check the use of power-based, unilateral trade policy making – that is, the weaponization of trade. And, as Mavroidis and Sasmal acknowledge, with the Appellate Body now in abeyance (see below) – and given the increasing heterogeneity of WTO members and growing economic nationalism – the risk of abuse of this Article (plus Article XX, to be considered in the next chapter) is substantial.

The scale and range of US unilateral measures in 2018 was unprecedented – greater even than that of the infamous Smoot–Hawley tariffs of 1930 that heralded the Depression (Khandelwal and Fajgelbaum 2022) – as is their longevity, most of the measures having been retained under the Biden administration. The US action did not, however, come out of the blue. The United States has a longstanding concern about the perceived constraints on its sovereignty imposed by WTO disciplines.

A particular focus of US dissatisfaction is a 2011 Appellate Body ruling, in *US – AD/CVD (China)*, that a majority government stake in an enterprise does not automatically constitute a 'public body' and therefore bestow the right to apply defensive duties on imports supported by government subsidies. This is part of a broader US concern that sees the Appellate Body Secretariat as having developed a jurisprudence that is openly hostile to trade defence instruments. A major outcome of US dissatisfaction is the blocking of the appointment of new judges to the Appellate Body in response to alleged judicial overreach in its rulings that has, according to the office of the United States Trade Representative, diminished WTO members' rights.[8] America's dissatisfaction with the WTO dispute settlement mechanism more generally will only be sharpened by the panel rulings in December 2022 against the Trump administration's steel and aluminium tariffs.

But we need to be clear that the question arising here is not whether US concerns are justified but, rather, the nature of America's remedial action. The 2021 WTO Trade Policy Review of China (WTO 2021c) highlights the areas of harmony but also areas of discord that inevitably arise in the complex trade relationship with China (see box 4).

Box 4 Trade Policy Review of China: a mixed bag

Extracts from Chair's Summary

- Recalling that 2021 marks the 20th anniversary of China's WTO accession, Members praised its active participation in, and commitment to, the WTO. In particular, Members welcomed its constructive participation in the Joint Statement Initiatives and

plurilateral discussions. Many Members also recognized China's participation in regional integration and took note of its growing network of free trade agreements.
- Noting that China benefited enormously from the multilateral trading system, some Members urged it to assume more responsibility commensurate to its trade weight to uphold and defend WTO principles.
- Members applauded China for unilaterally reducing MFN applied tariffs on a wide range of products. China was encouraged to continue tariff liberalization initiatives, particularly on agricultural products where tariffs were considered to be still relatively high.
- It was also widely commended for its various other measures to facilitate trade and reduce overall customs clearance times as well as for fully implementing the WTO's Trade Facilitation Agreement ahead of schedule.
- On investment, Members recognized China's steps to create a more attractive investment environment and welcomed recent liberalization in financial services and the negative list approach China had begun to adopt. However, various Members indicated that foreign companies established in China still reported significant issues relating to unequal treatment with local companies, inconsistent application of regulations, hidden subsidies, and business environment that was perceived as increasingly politicized.
- China was commended for the delivery of COVID-19 vaccines, for providing preferential tariff treatment to LDCs [least developed countries], for its ongoing participation in the Aid for Trade Initiative, and for its overall engagement in South–South cooperation.
- For many Members, the lack of transparency with regard to China's state measures was an issue of fundamental concern. Members noted a generally opaque subsidy regime and the lack of timely

notifications on key issues such as state-trading enterprises and domestic support and encouraged China to submit these notifications. Members underlined that transparency was a fundamental WTO principle and urged China to fully comply with its transparency commitments.
- Many Members highlighted the importance of SOEs [state-owned enterprises] in China's economy and expressed concerns about implicit support to SOEs and distortions created by them. In this context, Members recalled China's accession commitments and urged it to speed up reforms and fully embrace market-oriented policies.
- Members expressed support for China's efforts to promote the use of clean energy and the recent establishment of a carbon emission trading system, with a view to decarbonizing its economy.
- Several Members raised concerns about China's SPS regime, including that emergency measures taken in the context of the COVID-19 pandemic were without scientific justification and that new regulations to be introduced on overseas producers of imported food were unclear and potentially trade restrictive.
- Some Members also voiced concerns over a general increase in non-transparent and discriminatory measures and practices in China, sometimes in response to political disagreements with other trading partners. They urged China to take measures to end non-transparent and discriminatory measures.
- Other issues of concern for some Members included: continuously insufficient IPR protection, laws and regulations related to cyber security and data management, a very wide definition of national security, insufficient measures to address steel overcapacity, and the use of forced labour in China's economy.
- With respect to fisheries, Members were encouraged by China's recent initiatives, including the termination

> of its own subsidy programmes as well as its indication that it will not seek full special and differential treatment in negotiations on fisheries subsidies. China's intention to crack down on Illegal, Unreported and Unregulated fishing was also welcomed and China was asked to ensure its controls are effective.

Within its measured diplomatic language, the chair's Trade Policy Review summary conceals the starkness of some of China's more egregious trade policies. One example is the $41 billion in cotton subsidies expended by China over the past decade – six times the US outlay and highly damaging to cotton-dependent farmers in sub-Saharan Africa. As we saw in chapter 1, when subsidies are combined with human rights abuses, as with treatment of the Uyghur population, then even penalty sanctions will be warranted. But what the review also reveals is that there are many fruitful areas of cooperation, and progress, in the relationship with China. Engagement within the WTO offers the opportunity both to pursue that cooperation and to confront China where its policies are lacking.

So, we are not questioning the US right to seek redress. The question rather is whether US action – taken unilaterally and in breach of its tariff bindings – is conducive to the good order and effective functioning of the WTO-based trading system. The point being made here is that trade relations conducted under duress, on a unilateral basis, are not sustainable. They also risk being emulated, as we shall now see by looking at some ongoing developments in Brussels.

The European Union

There is a growing view in Brussels and EU national capitals that Europe is ill equipped to defend itself, and its sovereignty, against inequities in global trade and that, by implication, the WTO rules cannot be relied upon to provide that defence, particularly now that the WTO dispute settlement system has stopped functioning. The result is a series of new trade defensive measures in the process of implementation. They all derive from unilateral, EU-based authority and have, at best, uncertain compatibility with WTO jurisprudence. These proposals have been the subject of close examination by Fredrik Erixon and his colleagues at the European Centre for International Political Economy (Erixon et al. 2022b). We will look at five of them, first describing their scope then, in the next section, considering the risks they entail.

Anti-Coercion Instrument (ACI) – The legal basis for this initiative is Article 207 of the Treaty on the Functioning of the European Union. The ACI is designed to deter and counteract coercive actions, seen as violating EU sovereignty, by third countries through the use of the EU's own trade defence arsenal.[9] Measures to be deployed under the ACI include the suspension of tariff concessions, the imposition of customs duties and restrictions on the importation of goods, limits on access to the EU's public procurement market, and suspensions in trade in services and trade-related aspects of intellectual property rights. Where proposed action would be inconsistent with the EU's WTO obligations, it would simply invoke the national security exception under Article XXI. Ultimately, says the European Commission, the goal is to reinforce the EU's strategic autonomy and effectively protect the interests of the EU and its member countries (European Commission 2021).

International Procurement Initiative (IPI) – The IPI is designed to leverage market access in procurement markets in favour of EU firms and to restrict access to the EU's procurement market for companies from countries where EU companies face restrictive or discriminatory measures in public procurement. It imposes score adjustments, which act as penalties that procurement authorities have to apply to a company subject to the IPI, and the exclusion of tenders from designated third countries and sectors subject to the IPI. The potential scope and range of this measure is considerable. It could, for example, cover activities comparable to a water project being undertaken in Poland by a Chinese firm, valued at €53 million, or a gas pipeline in Romania under construction by a Turkish contractor valued at €127 million.

Foreign Subsidy Instrument (FSI) – The legal basis for this instrument comes from articles 207 and 114 of the Treaty on the Functioning of the European Union. The FSI is designed to address the distortive effects of foreign subsidies granted to overseas-owned firms operating within the EU market – something which, it is claimed, current legislation prevents the EU from doing. Under the FSI the EU Commission can impose redressing measures, such as reduced market access, on companies using foreign subsidies in mergers and acquisitions, public procurement or other market situations when operating within the EU. A particular EU concern is that foreign companies benefiting from subsidies become dominant when operating within the EU market and abuse their dominance by engaging in unfair trade practices. Sectors with a higher prevalence of foreign subsidiaries are more likely to be impacted by the FSI. This would include steel and aluminium, aviation, railways (in the context of public procurement for infrastructure), oil and gas, and semiconductors. A particular motivation for this measure is that China has become the fourth largest purchaser of EU undertakings, bringing with it a perceived lack of operational transparency.

Level Playing Field in the EU–UK Trade and Cooperation Agreement (LPF) – The LPF establishes rules to safeguard fair competition between EU and British businesses by ensuring that there is no regression from current standards maintained between the EU and the UK that could distort trade and provide either of them with a more competitive edge. Under the LPF, the UK or the EU can impose redressive measures if the other changes its labour or environmental regulations to provide an unfair advantage to their companies.

The Updated Enforcement Regulation for Trade Disputes (ER) – The domestic legal basis for this initiative (which came into force in February 2021) rests on articles 133 and

308 of the Treaty Establishing the European Community and Article 207 of the Treaty on the Functioning of the European Union. Under the ER, the EU can take countermeasures when Europe's interests are considered to be at risk by a failure to implement a panel in the WTO because of paralysis in the Appellate Body or when a similar situation arises under another international trade agreement. All sectors can be subject to the Updated Enforcement Regulation, including trade in services and matters relating to intellectual property rights.

The price of unilateral application of trade defence

The pursuit of trade remedies on a unilateral basis, in the name of national sovereignty, carries a high price not only for the countries targeted but also for the users of the weapon and for the framework of cooperation on which world trade depends.

The United States: the Trump tariffs

As a unilateral measure, the steel and aluminium tariffs were perceived generally as being unclear, unpredictable and arbitrary, leading to major uncertainty about the level of the tariff, its timeframe and the scope of its product and – of particular importance – its country coverage. On this last point, the experience of Canada is instructive. The punitive tariff on aluminium was lifted for imports from Canada in May 2019, reimposed in August 2020 and eliminated again in September 2020.

It was clear from the outset that this use of the trade weapon would neither meet its stated objective nor yield net benefit to the United States. Imposing penalty tariffs on steel and aluminium was never going to enhance US national security. At the time the measures were imposed, the American defence industry took only 3 per cent of US steel production, and over 80 per cent of US steel imports came from allies – China accounting for only 2 per cent. Nor did the tariffs address the underlying problem of excess global steel capacity. As to the US aluminium industry, its problems were very largely of its own making, with the US International Trade Commission finding that, at least for unwrought aluminium, the industry's handicap was self-imposed as a result of limited investments in smelting technologies during a period of declining prices (ITC 2017).

The penalty tariffs on steel and aluminium also serve as a practical illustration of the self-harm that comes from the use of the trade weapon. It has been estimated that American steel users now pay an extra $650,000 per year for every steel job saved (Hufbauer et al. 2022) and that, for each of those jobs saved in steel and aluminium from US tariffs, sixteen would be lost elsewhere.[10] And when retaliation from trading partners is taken into account the costs become even greater, as witnessed by the expressions of concern from US farm lobbies and carmakers at Chinese restrictions on imports from the United States, expressly targeted at Trump voters.

Moreover, the distortions to US imports of steel and aluminium did not – as noted above – disappear with the presidency of Joe Biden. This, again, can be seen as a practical illustration of the risks of protectionist capture. In 2021 and 2022, the Biden administration reached deals to replace certain steel and aluminium tariffs with tariff rate quota systems, whereby specified levels of imports will not face tariffs, but imports above the thresholds will. Tariff rate quotas for the European Union took effect in January 2022, for Japan in April 2022 and for the United Kingdom in June 2022. According to modelling by the Tax Foundation (a fiscally conservative think tank based in Washington, DC), tariffs remaining in place under the Biden administration will reduce long-run US GDP by 0.22 per cent ($55.7 billion) and wages by 0.14 per cent and eliminate 173,000 full-time equivalent jobs.

The European Union: the new battery of trade remedies

Each of the trade remedy measures being implemented in the EU carries both a major retaliatory risk and a threat to the cooperative framework of trade rules and its core principles of non-discrimination, coherence and proportionality. Economic modelling by Amar Breckenridge and his colleagues shows that, together, these measures will stifle EU trade and impose a major brake on EU growth and development (Breckenridge et al. 2022).

The Anti-coercion Instrument (ACI)
As the ECIPE paper makes clear, legal complications could arise with the ACI because of ambiguities, both in defining economic coercion and in the assignment of a remedy. For example, although the ACI regulation takes into account non-conventional forms of diplomatic coercion – such as cyber-attacks, debt traps and boycotts, there is still uncertainty about the type of response in such cases. The inclusion of IPR provisions also creates uncertainty, as the EU cannot suspend the rights of a country in international IPR conventions in the same way it could suspend concessions in a trade agreement. As to potential targets, discussions with EU Commission officials have indicated that China and the United States are the principal targets, with, for the US, sanctions policy a primary concern – for example, Iran sanctions and Nord Stream 2 sanctions. The potential for discord – with an ally – is abundantly clear.

The risk of retaliation against ACI measures is very high and will depend in part on the difficult task facing the EU of not making ACI measures disproportionate to the coercion identified. For example, it would be a highly complex matter to determine the cost to an EU company of China's slowing down its internet connection. Should the ACI measure seem arbitrary or disproportionate, the risk of escalation in trade tension is very real.

The International Procurement Initiative (IPI)
The scope for disputation is considerable with the IPI, as there has been a steady rise in the number of protectionist measures imposed by countries in their procurement markets. In 2021, there were 260 discriminatory procurement measures, ten times the number of measures in 2009. The

worst offenders are the United States, India and Russia, accounting for more than half of the world's restrictive procurement measures.¹¹

The risk of retaliation against use of the IPI will be heightened by the fact that, while the EU is a major beneficiary of overseas procurement contracts, EU member states themselves impose restrictions on their public procurement markets and also that the EU's share of global imports in procurement is relatively low, with the proportion of contracts awarded to foreign companies representing under 5 per cent of the EU procurement market.

Foreign Subsidy Instrument (FSI)
Again, with the FSI the scope for disputation is great, given the increase in foreign subsidies granted to overseas-owned firms operating in the EU – rising by almost 40 per cent in 2020.¹² The risk of retaliation against the FSI has been considerably augmented by the recent relaxation of EU competition policy, which now allows – in total contradiction with the spirit of the FSI – state subsidies for Important Projects of Common European Interest, under which EU member states will support the development of specific sectors such as microelectronics and electric batteries and in all likelihood extending in future to electric vehicles, smart health, low-carbon industries, hydrogen technologies, the industrial Internet of Things and cyber security. And, on top of all this, under the EU Chips Act, and as noted earlier, the EU has earmarked €11 billion in subsidies to foster the production of semiconductors in Europe.

Inevitably, much of the production of these subsidized activities will find its way into cars, machinery or electronic products where EU firms are leading exporters – thus providing easy targets for retaliation against EU subsidies and the unilateral penalties imposed under the FSI.

Level Playing Field (LPF)
In principle, the scope for retaliation against the LPF provisions is limited, as any disputation between the EU and the UK would be dealt with under the dispute settlement

provisions of the Trade and Cooperation Agreement between the two parties. Nevertheless, given the proclivity for cross-channel irritation, the possibility of retaliation being taken outside of the agreement – thus putting the whole agreement at risk – cannot be totally ruled out.

The Updated Enforcement Regulation for Trade Disputes (ER)

How the Enforcement Regulation works in particular cases will depend on whether the country with which the EU is in dispute (country X) is one of the fifty-three members of the Multiparty Interim Appeal Arbitration Agreement (MPIA) – the replacement for the frozen WTO appeal body. Where country X is, like the EU, a member of the MPIA, the ER will only be triggered if that party fails to comply with the MPIA ruling. Where country X is not a member of the MPIA, the EU will turn directly to the Enforcement Regulation to implement the appropriate counter-measures or suspend concessions to country X.

Although EU officials claim that the ER neither diminishes the role of the WTO nor stands in the way of WTO modernization, the WTO dispute settlement understanding does not provide for unilateral action in the event of a non-solution to a panel report that has been appealed. It is quite possible therefore that counter-measures taken by the EU under the Updated Enforcement Regulation for Trade Disputes will be challenged as discriminatory either under the Most Favoured Nation or the National Treatment provisions of the GATT.

The risk of retaliation against ER measures is particularly high because the regulation itself targets disputed cases without waiting for a resolution. The retaliatory risk will be especially elevated where a country targeted by the ER is not a member of the MPIA and could well respond with its own counter-measures. India, the United States, Argentina and Russia are not part of the MPIA and traditionally have been the subject of a large number of EU dispute cases.

As if all this were not enough, making the ER operational for trade in services, say in banking or retail activities, will entail considerable uncertainty and complexity. This is because, for services trade, where there is no common external tariff, individual EU members retain considerable autonomy in their liberalization commitments. Thus, if the EU were to impose trade restrictions in services, the same measure would have different consequences – and costs – in terms of market access restrictions across the EU. This could well add discord among EU member states to the inevitable discord between the EU and its trading partners that will arise from the application of the Updated Enforcement Regulation. Similar complexities are likely to arise in the application of the ER to intellectual property rights.

Given the high cost – to user and target – of unilateral use of the trade weapon as a trade remedy, the question arises: Are there not alternative ways of reconciling the pursuit of national sovereignty with compliance with international rules providing redress and relief within the trading system? In fact, a better approach to trade remedies calls for action not just at the international level, within the WTO, but also at the national and regional levels. We will now look at each of these three aspects in turn.

A better way: some implications for policy makers

A more holistic domestic policy approach to trade defence

To restrain use of the trade weapon in power-based, unilateral trade defence, a basic requirement is that, at the national level, governments take a more holistic approach to trade remedies – considering the economy-wide effects of redressing trade measures beyond the interests of the industries seeking relief – themselves subject to the dynamics of protectionist capture. In the case of the Trump–Biden steel tariffs, this means – or would have meant – taking account of the interests of steel users as well as steel producers.

However, given the political economy of trade protection, pursuit of such an economy-wide perspective – however necessary – will take time and will need to be backed by collective efforts at the regional and multilateral level.

Regional cooperation and the use of competition policy

Competition policy is closely associated with trade remedies insofar as some parties to preferential trade agreements have agreed to forgo anti-dumping action against each other and rather rely on their respective competition authorities to monitor and, as necessary, discipline dumping.

All the preferential agreements of the European Free Trade Association contain provisions dealing with competition policy, and three of the more recent agreements (with Singapore, Chile and Korea) provide for the abolition of anti-dumping measures between the parties. Since 1990, Australia and New Zealand have, under their Closer Economic Relations agreement, opted to use their respective competition policies as an alternative to taking anti-dumping action against one another.[13]

However, replacing anti-dumping action with treatment under cooperating countries' competition law is not a viable option for the many developing countries that lack a fully operational competition law and competition authority. So, it is significant that neither of the two current-generation preferential agreements in the Asia-Pacific, the Regional Comprehensive Economic Partnership (RCEP) and the Comprehensive and Progressive Trans-Pacific Partnership (CPTPP), contain provisions for dealing with dumping, or any other form of trade remedy, through competition policy. Action multilaterally must be part of the solution.

Restoring the judicial authority of the WTO

Finding an alternative to the unilateral application of trade remedies requires that the dispute-resolution authority of the WTO be more firmly asserted (as part of a broader WTO revival that we will look at in chapter 5).[14] In the interim, there is the provisional MPIA arrangement, but big traders such as Britain, India, Russia, South Korea and the United States have not joined up, and it is being used in only a relatively small number of dispute cases.

There is no magic wand, however, for restoring the WTO's judicial authority, even though the common – and serious

– assertion that the organization suffers from a democratic deficit lacks credibility. Let's see why not, exploring three related questions formulated by Robert Howse.[15]

Do WTO rules lack democratic consent?
WTO negotiation entails a principal–agent relationship whereby the authority to negotiate is vested by government in trade officials, with the attendant risks of both uneven access to what's going on ('information asymmetries') and of differences of interest between agents and principals. The fear arising is that the traditional way of dealing with these 'agency costs', through ex post legislative control, is too late and too permissive, particularly when a complex package is presented that must be accepted or rejected by the legislature in its totality.

In response to this fear, it may be said that, with the now predominant focus on issue-by-issue negotiation (given the demise of the 'single undertaking' covering a wide range of topics), the task of legislative overview has become less complex. There is, nevertheless, the option of accompanying ex post review with the imposition of ex ante negotiating conditions. The danger with that, though, is of limiting the agent's options and hence the chance of reaching agreement at the international level.

Are WTO rules democracy-undermining?
As the notion of 'market access' has been broadened to take in behind-the-border domestic regulation, concerns arise that governments' right to regulate in sensitive areas such as education, the environment or public health is being compromised and that in other areas, such as the protection of intellectual property rights, the interests of multinational corporations are being placed ahead of those of the community at large.

Counter-arguments here include the fact that, in the area of trade in services, the right to regulate is firmly asserted in the GATS framework, as is the option of not 'scheduling' any particular sector for liberalization commitments. And, in the equally sensitive area of sanitary and phytosanitary regulation, the insistence under WTO rule-making on 'science-based' approaches is designed to reduce the risk of arbitrary outcomes.

Do WTO actors fail to practise democratic political ethics?
The GATT–WTO has been characterized as having a 'club' atmosphere that is antithetical to the core of democratic political ethics embodied in inclusiveness, transparency and value pluralism. Here, again, counter-arguments can be advanced. The GATT–WTO system has evolved into a genuinely multilateral process in which a wider range of both state and non-state actors are engaged. Transparency has been improved as WTO documentation has become more readily available, the Trade Policy Review mechanism has extended its scope, and amicus curiae (friends of the court) briefs have come to inform WTO dispute settlement proceedings. And while WTO values remain firmly set on combating protectionism, the pursuit of this objective draws together major players as diverse in their value pluralism as the United States, China, Russia and India.

There is, however, the rather special case of the less advanced developing countries – is the 'club' sufficiently mindful of their needs? The former WTO director general Pascal Lamy thought not, calling for the rules of the trading system to be 'more development friendly'.[16] A case in point is the very limited resort to the dispute settlement system by the least developed countries, largely because the bulk of their trade benefiting from developed country preferences is unbound and therefore not part of enforceable WTO law. Even here, however, the primary need is for reduced developing country dependence on preferences,[17] backed by facilities such as Aid for Trade.

In drawing together the strands of the democratic deficit argument, it needs to be acknowledged that the activities of any international organization will inevitably involve trade-offs between competing objectives: between accountability and efficiency and between institutional authority and national sovereignty – our principal focus in this chapter. Within individual issue areas there will also be difficult trade-offs; the paradox of patents, for example, involves restricting access to knowledge today in order to improve it in future.

In seeking to find the right balance between these conflicting priorities, the WTO is in constant evolution, as seen by the decision of the twelfth WTO Ministerial Conference (MC12) to waive certain COVID-19 vaccine IPRs. And, as long as it is, this must be seen as the strongest safeguard against incurring a 'democratic deficit'.

Closing thoughts

However persuasive the defence of the WTO's democratic credentials, this in itself will not bring the United States back to the table or restrain the resort of the US – and, indeed, the EU – to the unilateral, power-based pursuit of trade remedies in the name of national sovereignty.

For America in particular, restoring faith in multilateral rules means re-establishing confidence that the WTO dispute settlement mechanism can effectively adjudicate and defend the use of trade remedies under WTO authority. On the face of it, the Appellate Body ruling that a majority government stake in an enterprise does not automatically constitute a public body does seem incongruous.

A possible way of getting round this might be to adopt the approach to state-owned enterprises (SOEs) that is now taken in the Comprehensive and Progressive Trans-Pacific Partnership, of which China is an aspiring member. CPTPP contains hard law commitments and the threat of suspension of equivalent concessions in the event of a breach, seen as signalling a new strategy to discipline SOEs through trade law commitments as distinct from antitrust principles.[18] This does, however, seem to be a rather fine distinction, and, at a more practical level, what can be said with some confidence is that, for disciplines on SOEs to be accepted, compromise will be needed. One element of such a compromise would be an undertaking from China to end subsidies for SOEs operating in competitive markets abroad, in return for more tolerance for those supplying public services within China. But, in addition to the trading majors, action is also needed – including through Aid for Trade – to enable developing countries to play a more active role in the judicial, as well as rule-making, arms of the trading system.

Only in this way, by maximizing the number of rule-respecting players within the trading system, and especially the big players, will it be possible to resolve the underlying conundrum of how to secure the sovereignty of the individual within the collective body. Put simply, you get back as much as you put in. Jean-Jacques Rousseau, though writing 233 years before the WTO was formed, nevertheless hit the nail on the head and gives us a still valid guiding principle:

> Finally, each man in giving himself to all, gives himself to nobody; and as there is no associate over whom he does not acquire the same right as he yields others over himself, he gains an equivalent for everything he loses, and an increase of force for preservation of what he has.

This helpful guideline has been repeated in comparable terms, more recently, by the philosopher John Rawls.[19]

A practical illustration of the importance of the force of numbers in WTO dispute settlement jurisprudence came in 2012, when Japan lodged a complaint in the WTO against China for having blocked exports to it of rare earth minerals crucial to many of Japan's technology firms. Japan responded by lodging a complaint against China in the WTO. Crucially, it managed to persuade the United States and the European Union to join in the appellate process. In the face of this trade diplomacy, China backed down. But, of course, China, in this case, was obliged to back down. So, reconciling the conundrum of sovereignty within a collective body does not mean that individual players will never lose a disputed case. But when individual WTO members do give way, they do so within a framework of agreed rules that, as is worth repeating, are non-discriminatory, coherent and proportionate.

These are the three principles that will need to illuminate the path to restored trust in the rules-based trading order, without which it will be an uphill struggle to check the co-option of trade policy for the pursuit of other goals, the subject of our next chapter, when looking at the battle for science.

4
Battling for the Greater Good

The trade weapon, such as Europe's Carbon Border Adjustment Mechanism, is being used, ostensibly, to promote the climate transition by trying, as Brussels would see it, to punish environmental free-riders. But, by fostering discord and confusion, it will end up doing more harm than good.

Trade in essential solar photovoltaic materials, such as polysilicon, is critical to the climate transition by enabling the conversion of sunlight into electricity, and yet – as countries attempt to develop national capacity – this trade is being severely constrained by extensive tariff and non-tariff barriers. Moreover, while trade is a key multiplier in spreading the technology vital to the climate transition, protectionist tendencies embedded in the implementation of that transition pose a threat not only to realizing the benefits of individual climate-related initiatives but also to the global trading system itself, and hence to climate action more broadly.

An equally negative dynamic is at work in the field of public health. In chapter 2 we saw how the disruption caused by the COVID-19 pandemic has contributed to concerns about supply-chain dependence. In this chapter we will see how concerns about the virus itself, and national attempts to deal with it, have led to trade policies that, again, are self-defeating and how, two years into the pandemic, WTO members continued to have export restrictions, with a trade value of $122 billion, on products that were essential to combat the disease – such as bioreactor bags, crucial to the vaccine supply chain.

But it is not enough just to say 'no' to the invocation of trade restrictions. Fortunately, there are other ways in which more expansive, open trade policies can make a genuine contribution to tackling these compelling, and growing, environmental and public health challenges.

Damaging use of the trade weapon

The climate transition

Trade, technology and the climate transition
Technological innovation – backed by a carbon tax to make it competitive – is the essential requirement for transition to net-zero carbon emissions by 2050. And trade, by stimulating competition, is a catalyst of innovation. Three areas of technological transformation stand out.

The first is solar photovoltaic technology that uses solar panels to convert sunlight into electricity. Over the past decade, solar photovoltaic has become a pillar of the low-carbon sustainable energy system, with installed capacity increasing one hundredfold and costs declining by 77 per cent. Some 40 per cent of the decline in the cost of solar photovoltaic modules since 2001 is attributable to trade (WTO and IRENA 2021). The second area of trade-augmented innovation is the export of low-carbon hydrogen, important in hard-to-electrify sectors such as steel production and facing a potential sixfold increase in demand by 2050. Australia is at the forefront in using renewable energy to produce zero-emissions ammonia – a low-cost carrier for hydrogen – and no fewer than six Japanese corporations have hydrogen development projects in Australia (Armstrong 2021). The third area of innovation is CRISPR (clustered regularly interspaced short palindromic repeats). This gene-editing helps countries decarbonize their food systems by making export crops that are resistant to disease or bad weather, reducing the need for increased farmland via deforestation – the source of 10 per cent of global carbon emissions. CRISPR-based genome editing of oil palm to eradicate basal stem rot will significantly reduce plant loss and subsequent compensatory deforestation in Indonesia and Malaysia – the leading exporters of palm oil. A switch to trade in gene-edited palm oil promises major environmental benefits.[1]

Beyond trade's multiplier role in spreading the benefits of specific technologies such as these, it also has a more general function in stimulating the economic growth necessary to fund the energy transformation – but also to bring down CO_2 emissions. For while emissions rise during the transition to affluence, they then flatten and eventually fall. The need is for more growth, not, as some now advocate,[2] less. As growth proceeds, the rate of carbon emissions, eventually, falls. In America, emissions fell by 15 per cent between 2007 and 2019, as GDP per person rose by 23 per cent.[3] In Europe, emissions fell by 30 per cent between 1980 and 2019. The decoupling of growth and emissions has also occurred in some developing countries, with Mexico's emissions falling by 16 per cent since their peak in 2012. This effect can be seen as an Environmental Kuznets Curve, comparable with the observation of the economist Simon Kuznets, described in the introduction, that the wealth gap increases as growth proceeds, before flattening and then falling.[4]

The decoupling of GDP growth and the rate of carbon emissions occurs for two reasons: first, when output becomes less energy intensive as activity shifts from manufacturing to less polluting services; and, second, when the energy used becomes cleaner. Most of the decoupling that has been observed – affecting some thirty-three countries in total – is the result of the first effect. Importantly, there is a trade dimension to this shift, as countries to which manufacturing activity has been outsourced are now emitting less carbon themselves. In China, for example, the export sector has decarbonized faster than the rest of the economy. This effect is mirrored in US consumption emissions, which measures the carbon embedded in imports, and which have also fallen between 2007 and 2019.

At a global level, however, because of continued high emissions in a number of developing countries, notably China and India, the decoupling so far observed has not been enough to reduce the world's carbon emissions. Hence the pressing need to address the second contributor to decoupling – the greening of the energy used to generate growth.

Yet despite trade's key role in the climate transition, the transition itself threatens trade and hence climate action. This threat arises because, as the environmental commitment varies between countries – as it inevitably will – pressure mounts for tariff restrictions on imports of carbon-intensive products, such as steel, from perceived environmental free-riders.

However, the difficulty of identifying carbon intensity and free-riding fuels the view that such penalties are simply disguised protectionism. The resulting tensions – augmented by the climate transition's emotive power and by broader protectionist tendencies, including as countries favour their own climate technologies – pose a major threat to the trading system.

The carbon border tax is central to this danger. Let's see how.

Carbon border taxes
Some prominent economists, such as William Nordhaus, Thomas Piketty and Jean Tirole, are advocating the imposition of carbon border taxes on imports from polluting countries. Such calls are founded on the fear that levies on carbon-intensive production simply push production to countries where it is not taxed. There is, however, no evidence of growth in pollution havens (OECD 2017). The International Energy Agency (IEA) reports that, already by 2019, global energy-related CO_2 emissions had flattened, with strong renewables growth in both China – looking to reduce oil-import dependence – and India. China, Japan and South Korea have each set target dates for zero net carbon emissions.

Compounding the pollution-haven misperception is the underlying problem that trade restrictions (whatever their motivation) carry the risk of protectionist capture and of being a brake on the economic growth and development needed to pay for the transition to cleaner energy.

The risk of protectionist capture is particularly apparent in the writings of some economists. In a recent publication, the former World Bank chief economist Joseph Stiglitz, together with colleagues from the Roosevelt Institute, speaks approvingly of a proposed global arrangement between the United States and the European Union on sustainable steel and aluminium that would decarbonize two heavy carbon emitting industries (Stiglitz et al. 2022). The agreement, the authors say, would herald a novel departure from 'decades of dogmatic trade policy that surrendered undue power to the market', and that would 'save good union jobs at home while having an objectively verifiable benefit in the battle against climate change.' In criticizing reliance on the price mechanism, the strong implication is that steel and aluminium designated as dirty would be subject not to border tariffs but to more draconian quantitative restrictions.

This risk is real: carbon border adjustments are becoming an integral part of EU trade policy. To use a mantra much loved in Brussels, this is indeed 'a Europe that protects'.[5] On 14 July 2021, EU officials announced a plan to phase out production subsidies and free pollution permits that had been issued to selected dirty industries, replacing them with a 'carbon border adjustment mechanism' (CBAM). CBAM – or, as Paul Krugman would have it, See? Bam![6] – requires firms to purchase pollution certificates when importing products from countries with perceived lax environmental standards. The mechanism in effect imposes tariffs on exporters of carbon-intensive products from countries without strong carbon mitigation regimes.

The plan – the legal basis for which would be Articles 191 to 193 of the Treaty on the Functioning of the European Union – is part of thirteen proposals from the European Commission aimed at cutting carbon emissions to 55 per cent below their 1990 level by 2030 and at achieving net zero by 2050. By imposing a carbon border tax and flexing its extra-territorial regulatory muscle, the European Union aims – in effect – to shift part of the burden of environmental reform onto foreign producers. The eventual outcomes and the extent of distortion to world trade are difficult to predict. Two key factors are in play: the extent to which affected exporters shift away from Europe towards other markets, and the extent to which they incorporate carbon costs in their exports or are deemed by the European Union to have done so.

The potential for impact on the Asia-Pacific region, in particular, is very real. The measures would see subsidies phased out and border protection implemented across six sectors: aluminium, cement, fertilizers, electricity, iron and steel, and hydrogen. These sectors all engage Asia-Pacific exporters, all of which are vulnerable to increased trade costs in accessing the EU market or negative displacement effects in third-country markets as exports are redirected away from Europe.

The nature of the final CBAM package coming out of Brussels and the way it is implemented will be crucial. One suggestion made by Asia-Pacific stakeholders in a survey of business and government is that the revenue generated by the border tax be used to help developing countries advance their 'common but differentiated' decarbonization efforts. Indonesian participants stressed this point (Konrad Adenauer Stiftung 2021). But if EU border taxes are to be the trade-off for eliminating subsidies and free pollution permits, European stakeholders won't want the proceeds going to developing countries – not even the least developed, for whom no special provisions are being made in the CBAM proposal. The prospects are strong that part of the cost of EU environmental reform will be shifted – directly or indirectly – to a diverse range of countries in the Asia-Pacific.

The prospect of discrimination and protectionist outcomes seems inevitable given the fact that, during a critical transition period between the phasing in of CBAM in 2026 and the phasing out of free pollution permits in Europe in 2034, the EU will both impose a penalty tax on imports *and* continue to subsidize domestic pollution. This will add fuel to perceptions elsewhere that CBAM is simply opportunistic protectionism.

The prevailing view among Indian stakeholders is that the proposed EU CBAM is protectionist, with potentially damaging effects on small producers of steel and cement. While noting that China is introducing an emissions-trading scheme with assistance from the European Union, Chinese stakeholders expressed concern about disagreements over the CBAM escalating into another front in trade conflict. Conflict in fact is unavoidable given the difficulty (and cost) of measuring the carbon emitted by taxable imports[7] – especially those within complex supply chains – and establishing how far foreign governments have already taxed such emissions.

Interlocutors in Brussels have indicated that countries would be exempted from CBAM if they have equivalent climate change policies to the EU and that America could dodge the levies on that basis. But what is 'equivalent'? The European Commission seems only to include a direct payment for carbon emissions in its scope for carbon costs that can be deducted. This is unlikely to hold up, as many producers of CBAM goods in third countries pay broad carbon taxes and other forms of non-direct levies for their carbon emissions, and it would be unfair to exclude those. Moreover, measuring the amount of carbon emitted and the carbon tax already paid without discriminating between countries, as required by the World Trade Organization, will be even more difficult. Potential claims are that CBAM is:

- in breach of the non-discrimination commitment, as it discriminates between like products;
- in breach of the national treatment obligation that imported products be given no less favourable treatment than that given to similar domestic products; and
- ineligible for exceptions under GATT Article XX because it cannot reference – as normally required – the support of a multilateral environment agreement for the specific action being taken, as the EU, as a signatory to the Paris Agreement, has accepted the national determined contributions to carbon-emissions reductions by other signatories.

Some countries, such as South Korea, will also challenge the compatibility of CBAM with commitments under EU preferential trade agreements.[8]

The ultimate risk of CBAM is that other governments decide to compensate their firms for CBAM costs, leading to growing, rather than diminishing, fossil fuel subsidies. Moreover, any environmental benefit, globally, from CBAM will be limited by the fact that, for all of the selected CBAM commodities, the EU is not the most important market for its major suppliers (Erixon et al. 2022).

And finally, perversely, given the amounts of foreign aluminium and iron and steel embedded in EU final demand and exports, CBAM will be more costly for those EU economies which are more integrated into the global economy, and costlier still as other countries retaliate against the imposts of CBAM. Such retaliation will become even likelier as the energy crisis triggered by the war in Ukraine prompts Germany to reverse plans to retire more than one-fifth of its coal-fired power stations; Austria, France and the Netherlands either to delay closure of or reopen coal plants; and the EU Commission to sell an extra 200 million carbon permits.[9]

Technology denied
Coming back to the three areas of technological promise outlined earlier, what we thus find – as a result of questionable environmentally weaponized border protection and broader protectionist forces – is that in each of these fields there are strong contradictory and damaging forces of trade restriction.

Trade in solar photovoltaic technology is subject to both tariff and non-tariff barriers. Some thirty-one WTO members apply protective tariffs over 10 per cent to certain essential solar photovoltaic materials such as polysilicon (WTO and IRENA 2021). Between 2011 and 2022, anti-dumping and countervailing impediments to solar photovoltaic products grew from just one to sixteen, with eight under consideration, covering 15 per cent of global demand outside China (IEA 2022). And the United States, since 2018, has restricted the import of solar panels from virtually all sources – even though only 14 per cent of US workers in the sector are in manufacture, the rest being in installation and R&D.[10]

Often, the red tape associated with trade restrictions compounds the damage. In the United States in the course of 2022, over 300 solar power projects were either delayed or cancelled because of federal probes into allegations of, in one case, evasion of US tariffs by solar panel and module manufacturers in Cambodia, Malaysia, Thailand and Vietnam and, in another case, circumvention of anti-dumping tariffs by Chinese companies.

And in a related area of green technology – the production of batteries for electric vehicles – the United States has introduced a blatantly protectionist provision under the Inflation Reduction Act, signed into law in August 2022 and authorizing (as we saw in chapter 2) some $400 billion in funding for energy-related projects. In order for new electric vehicles to qualify for a $7,500 purchase subsidy, half the components in its battery must come from the US, Canada or Mexico; by 2030, all of them will have to. The fear in the European Union, Japan and South Korea is that this measure will draw their companies into establishment within the United States. BMW, Toyota, Mercedes and Stellantis have all increased their FDI in the United States. And Emmanuel Macron has described the US subsidies as 'a killer for our industry'. The EU, which was contemplating WTO action against this measure, may get relief from the electric vehicle subsidy, but this would serve only to further fracture the world trading system.

The threat to trade in hydrogen comes from a call by competition-fearing European Union electricity groups for a carbon tariff on EU hydrogen imports. Though the case for Australia's blue hydrogen – using brown coal and carbon capture and storage – is controversial, the Carbon Border Adjustment Mechanism risks application to all hydrogen imports and a setback to carbon capture and storage, without which 'net zero' will be impossible.

And the threat to CRISPR gene-editing is a repeat of the type of regulatory barriers that invoke health and environmental concerns to hinder the development and trade of genetically modified organisms. Many countries' farming regulations, including those of New Zealand, constrain both GMOs and CRISPR, even though CRISPR does not introduce DNA from other species. The threat of continued restriction is particularly great in Europe. Both the track record of CRISPR and the underlying science argue in favour of its use as a safe and valuable innovation. Yet public concern, particularly in France, could yet see trade restrictions introduced in Europe at considerable cost to the environment and to global food supply.

In April 2021, the European Commission announced a proposed reform in the course of 2023 of the principle that gene-edited organisms are subject to the same assessment and labelling as any other genetically modified organism. The announcement prompted a report by the Greens/European Free Alliance (Greens/EFA) group in the European Parliament, expressing three concerns.[11]

Firstly, the report states that conflicts arise in the gene-editing work of three European research bodies – the European Plant Science Organization (EPSO), the EU network for Sustainable Agriculture through Genome Editing (EU-SAGE) and the European Federation of Academies of Sciences and Humanities – and that members of these bodies and the seed industry 'stand to benefit economically from a relaxation of the EU's GMO legislation.' Secondly, the Greens/EFA report expresses concern that most members of EPSO and EU-SAGE are experts in genetics and molecular biology, which it is claimed are less relevant to assessing potential negative consequences of using CRISPR in agriculture than, say, qualifications in ecology, socioeconomics or public health. Finally, the report asserts that the claims that gene editing is safe for the consumer and the environment are either false or highly misleading.

Shortly after its release the report received substantial press exposure, including in *Le Monde*, which reported that the trade union SUD-Recherche at the Institut national de recherche pour l'agriculture, l'alimentation et l'environnement (Inrae) was concerned about the links between Inrae and the three research bodies identified.[12]

Taking each of the concerns of the Greens/EFA report in turn, representatives of the three research bodies each claim full transparency and disclosure of interests on the part of their researchers. The charge of inapplicability of qualifications in genetics and molecular biology would seem hard to sustain. And thirdly – and most crucially – a principal incentive for using CRISPR is that it doesn't introduce genes from other organisms, such as bacteria. This means that the United States will not regulate CRISPR-based plants as genetically modified organisms (GMOs). Today the CRISPR-Cas9 enzyme is key to new treatments for sickle cell disease, hereditary blindness and several cancers. The discovery was honoured in 2020 by the Nobel Prize in Physiology to Jennifer Doudna of the University of California, Berkeley, and her French colleague Emmanuelle Charpentier.

Now, researchers at the Innovative Genomics Institute (IGI) in the United States hope to do for agriculture what CRISPR technology has already achieved in biomedical research – with the hope that most crops will be gene edited to some degree within the next ten to fifteen years. Collaborative research being undertaken by a group of highly reputed US institutions: the University of California at Berkeley and Davis, the Lawrence Livermore National Laboratory, the Howard Hughes Medical Institute and the IGI finds that suboptimal photosynthetic reactions in plants could be made between 20 per cent and 50 per cent more efficient. This means much more carbon captured from the earth.[13]

In Belgium, the Flanders Research Institute for Agriculture, Fisheries and Food is conducting field trials of genome-edited maize after greenhouse observations showed that the modified plants have improved growth during drought. In Japan, already in 2019, Hirhito Sone, an endocrinologist at Niigata University who chaired an expert panel into CRISPR use, said that there is little difference between traditional breeding methods and gene editing in terms of safety, paving the way for the sale of gene-edited foodstuffs to consumers in Japan.[14]

Hobbling the role of trade
In short, summing up our discussion so far, protectionism and protectionist capture, as well as reducing the growth-benefits of trade, are hobbling trade's role in fostering the technological promise of the climate transition – raising the level of the carbon tax needed to effect that transition and weakening public support for it. The stakes are particularly high for the WTO, which is about to face – via the climate transition and the ill-advised attack on alleged free-riders – one of the most severe systemic challenges in its history.

Few countries will want to change their environmental policies under duress, including under the threat of trade penalties. And, while the WTO (under Article XX) does allow measures necessary to protect human, animal or plant life, these provisions have rarely been used and, in the case of CBAM, may be inapplicable. Rather, what is needed is broader support for the principle that deficiencies in environmental policy should be addressed directly at their source and not through proxies in the form of weaponized trade. The European Union and the United States, in particular, should favour environmental policy such as by reducing fossil fuel subsidies and increasing public investment in green technology over pressure that distorts trade. We will return to this.

The COVID-19 virus

Impediments to trade
Trade continues to be a crucial element in the fight against the COVID-19 virus, and some countries, notably China, have sought to gain credit from providing vaccines to others, while cooperation through the COVAX initiative has seen vaccines shipped from India's Serum Institute to the poorest countries. Nevertheless, trade policy – and aggressive use of the trade weapon – has also been a serious impediment, at three levels: to the free flow of vaccines themselves, to the vital inputs for vaccine production, and to the knowledge behind their production.[15]

As of 12 May 2020, some ninety-two countries had imposed COVID-19-related export restrictions on medicines and medical products.[16] Some two years later, WTO members still had ninety-eight measures in place that prohibited or restricted exports as a result of the COVID-19 pandemic.[17] By the end of 2022, they continued to have export restrictions, with a trade value of $122 billion, on essential products to combat the spread of the disease. And they were, possibly, entirely within their rights, under WTO law, to do so (see box 5).

> **Box 5 Trade law and COVID-19-related export restrictions: plenty of wiggle room**
>
> GATT Article XI provides disciplines on export restrictions but, at paragraph 2a, explicitly permits export prohibitions or restrictions temporarily applied to prevent or relieve critical shortages of foodstuffs or other products essential to the exporting contracting party.
>
> The notion of 'critical shortages' was further elaborated by the WTO Appellate Body in the case of China–Raw Materials, as meaning 'deficiencies in quantity that are crucial, that amount to a situation of decisive importance, or that reach a vitally important or decisive stage, or a turning point.'
>
> One of the guiding principles in facilitating trade is the provision in GATT Article XI that any restrictions on export be temporary. We might note, however, that even a 'temporary' restriction can be highly disruptive within a complex global supply chain. Moreover, in addition to the wiggle room offered by Article XI, WTO law offers flexibility via Article XX – for restrictions 'necessary to protect human, animal or plant life or health' – and Article XXI – for 'any action which it considers necessary for the protection of its essential security interests.' There is nevertheless a transparency requirement, under Article XI, which provides that restrictions should be published promptly, enabling governments and traders to become acquainted with them.

> In short, if there is to be restraint in use of the trade weapon to limit access to critical vaccines or other medical supplies, then, beyond a basic requirement for transparency, we cannot rely on WTO trade law, as currently applied, to provide it.[18]

At critical times, therefore, various countries, including the United States, the European Union and India, have placed embargoes or administrative impediments on the export of vaccines themselves. China is in a somewhat unusual position in having effectively placed an embargo on vaccine import, refusing to purchase more effective Western mRNA vaccines, while relying, for a lengthy period, on an ill-conceived zero-COVID policy. The calamitous transition out of zero-COVID has highlighted the price paid by China for shunning the import of Western vaccines.[19]

Restrictions have also been placed – at a second level – on material needed for vaccine manufacture. By the end of April 2020, eighty countries had implemented export restrictions, and by November this number had increased to eighty-six (Bacchetta et al. 2021).

The invocation, in February 2021, by the United States of the Defense Production Act, which requires US suppliers of materials and equipment for vaccine production to seek approval to export, put at risk global access to thirty-seven critical items. The head of the Serum Institute of India, Adar Poonawalla, thus linked a global shortage of bioreactor bags – crucial in the vaccine supply chain – to the US policy of prioritizing domestic production. The potential for supply disruption is starkly apparent: as noted earlier, the Pfizer vaccine needs 280 components – including bioreactors, adjuvants and lipids – from eighty-six suppliers in nineteen countries.

A particular challenge in accessing vaccines and vaccine components, as pointed out by Chad Bown and Thomas Bollyky, is the need to overcome the reticence of developing countries that do not have the public health incentive to provide subsidies on a scale needed to satisfy global demand (Bown and Bollyky 2021). Such countries would only enjoy the 'externality' benefit of solving their own public health crisis if they were guaranteed access to other countries' vaccine output through trade. This has particular salience when looking at the challenge facing the poorest countries – a challenge, in fact, that, as we will now see, is shared by all.

Between mid-2020 and the end of 2021, 10 billion COVID-19 vaccine doses were produced, with global capacity to produce 12 billion doses a year. But distribution was highly uneven, with less than 1 per cent of the vaccines going to low-income countries. The World Health Organization's COVAX initiative fell well short of its target of delivering 2 billion doses to lower-middle and low-income countries by the end of 2021. And low-income countries had received barely 3 per cent of the $650 billion in special drawing rights issued for the International Monetary Fund's pandemic response.

The result – compounded by widespread vaccine hesitancy in poor countries – has been a high discrepancy in vaccination rates. By the end of 2022, Nigeria, for example, had fully vaccinated less than 25 per cent of its population, Papua New Guinea less than 4 per cent. Some 30 per cent of the world's population was yet to receive a single shot of a COVID-19 vaccine. But developing country vulnerability means global vulnerability. The Delta variant, first detected in India in April 2021 before becoming a world crisis, illustrates the danger of having large pockets of unvaccinated people.

Epidemiologists now warn that large swaths of the world may be inundated with new waves of COVID-19. As Abhijit Banerjee and Esther Duflo have observed, totally eliminating the virus seems to be a pipe dream – it simply has too many chances to multiply (Banerjee and Duflo 2022). There is, therefore, both an ethical and a self-interested reason for helping poorer countries cope with COVID-19 by improving their access to vaccines and vaccine components.

As to the third element of COVID-19-related restriction, knowledge, IPR restrictions continue to impede the acquisition by developing countries of knowledge of the new techniques involved in the design of vaccines and limit these countries' capacity to develop the cell lines needed in vaccine manufacture. Further ahead, the trade regime will need to be better aligned with the pursuit of knowledge to deal with future pandemics, including those arising from variants of SARS-CoV-2, against which current vaccines are likely to be less effective.

So, while we can welcome the decision of the twelfth WTO Ministerial Conference in June 2022 to a waiver under the Agreement on Trade Related Aspects of Intellectual Property Rights (TRIPS) allowing for the manufacture and export of COVID-19 vaccines without the consent of the patent holder, more far-reaching TRIPS reform should be possible without totally denying the paradox of patents – restricting knowledge now in order to increase it in the future. At the same time, it needs to be recognized that access to intellectual property is only one aspect of vaccine production, and not necessarily the most important.

Apart from the human suffering that has arisen from the weaponizing of trade in vaccines and vaccine products, there have been serious repercussions for the standing of different international actors and the values they represent. In Asia, the inability of many ASEAN countries to procure highly prized Western-manufactured Moderna and Pfizer vaccines in early 2021 meant strong recourse to the Chinese Sinopharm and Sinovac vaccines – accompanied by vaccine diplomacy in Beijing and in Moscow, suggesting that global public goods could be better addressed by centralized governance models.

Chinese and Russian vaccine diplomacy faces a serious reality check, given the lower effectiveness of Chinese vaccines, the non-recognition of Russian vaccines by certain health agencies, and the fact that while (as at end 2022) 96 per cent of China's 3.8 billion vaccine doses were sold, America's 623 million doses were donated.[20] This, however, will not necessarily translate into more trust in the European Union and the United States.

The handling of the COVID-19 pandemic and the way it has been perceived has thus dealt a serious reputational blow to the Western democracies. In Asia, for example, the EU is no longer seen as the champion of a rules-based international order, with trust dropping from 32.6 per cent in 2021 to 16.6 per cent in 2022 – just slightly ahead of China (ISEAS-Yusof Ishak Institute 2022). As Rosa Balfour and her colleagues at Carnegie Europe have put it, the initial retreat of the United States and the lacklustre performance of the European Union have given China and Russia free rein to consolidate their influence (Balfour et al. 2022).

So much for the shortcomings in the use of the trade weapon in response to environmental and public health challenges: time now to see how things might be done differently.

A better way: some implications for policy makers

The climate transition

Advocacy of protectionist use of the trade weapon ostensibly to promote the climate transition should be rebutted at every opportunity. It is not enough, however, just to say 'no' to trade impediments. The energy transition is not assured, and more needs to be done. China, Japan and Korea, notwithstanding their net zero emission targets and their, albeit faltering, movement in the right direction, still fund the majority of new coal-fired power plants. In China, measures to incentivise higher coal production were announced as part of the government's economic stimulus package in May 2022.

Fortunately, there are other trade-related measures that can be taken to serve environmental ends and which, importantly, involve reducing rather than increasing distortions to trade. Three such measures have been on the WTO agenda for some years but are proving frustratingly difficult to advance: attempts to reduce fishing subsidies, negotiations to liberalize trade in environmental goods and services, and the efforts of certain countries to ensure that gene-edited products are treated in the same way as conventional ones. While all this work should be maintained and encouraged – building on the commitment at MC12 to phase out fishing subsidies and expanding the environmental goods and services negotiations to cover the movement of environmental service providers – another issue warrants accelerated attention: work in the WTO to reduce subsidies encouraging the use of fossil fuels.

Fossil fuel subsidies
There are four plausible arguments for tackling fossil fuel subsidies in the WTO.[21]

First, the subsidies are very large, with associated risks to the climate. IMF studies suggest that complete elimination of fossil fuel subsidies would decrease global CO_2 emissions by 15 to 23 per cent (IMF 2016). Second, in the Marrakesh Agreement setting up the WTO, members recognize that their trade relations should allow for the optimal use of the world's resources in accordance with the objective of sustainable development. Third, under the Agreement on Subsidies and Countervailing Measures (ASCM), the WTO has a mandate to discipline the use of subsidies. And, fourth, a number of WTO disputes have targeted government policies that support the scaling up of renewable energy; so why not also target policies that support fossil fuel-based energy?

It is the last of these arguments, however, that prompts the first question about the applicability – or feasibility – of WTO engagement. The disputes involving renewable energy all have a clear trade dimension, usually involving claims of dumping. The use of domestic fossil fuel subsidies may not have such a clearly demonstrable trade dimension. This is because it is likely to be a difficult task to classify a domestic fossil fuel subsidy either as a prohibited or an actionable subsidy (which is specific and causes injury) under the ASCM.[22] If such a classification cannot readily be made, then the applicability of WTO dispute settlement becomes problematic given that, under ASCM rules, counter-measures under dispute settlement normally correspond to the value of trade injury incurred.

In light of this difficulty, an alternative approach that has been suggested[23] would be to tackle fossil fuel subsidies through the Anti-dumping Agreement by focusing on the widespread practice of dual pricing, whereby resource-endowed states sell their energy resources at significantly lower prices on the domestic market than on the export market. It would thus be argued that such dual pricing constitutes 'reversed input dumping' of products that benefit from below market energy prices, and which are therefore exported at less than 'normal value'. Again, however, there is uncertainty as to whether the Anti-dumping Agreement permits determining normal value in this manner.

Compounding these definitional problems is the fact that attempts to measure the scale of fossil fuel subsidies among bodies such as the International Energy Agency, the IMF and the OECD yield a daunting range of estimates – from $160 billion to $5.3 trillion (if negative externalities are included).

The second hurdle to concerted WTO engagement in the abolition of fossil fuel subsidies is that it would meet with strong opposition from developing countries that retain a high dependence on fossil fuels for their economic development. And, without the engagement of these countries, then even a fall-back plurilateral agreement among like-minded WTO members would be hardly feasible.

At the 2017 WTO Ministerial Conference in Buenos Aires, a group of twelve WTO members issued a ministerial statement calling on the WTO to achieve ambitious and effective disciplines on inefficient fossil fuel subsidies through enhanced WTO transparency and reporting. In the aftermath of MC12, forty-seven WTO members were actively participating in the Fossil Fuel Subsidy Reform Initiative; however, it does not yet seem ready for the negotiating agenda but, rather, to be concerned with mapping initiatives at the regional and national level. At a meeting of ministers from G20 countries in July 2021, officials from China, India, Russia and Saudi Arabia blocked an agreement to end fossil fuel subsidies. A breakthrough is not imminent.

Fortunately, as well as measures to reduce environmentally damaging distortions to trade, opportunities exist to foster under-exploited areas of trade that would help facilitate the climate transition. Four stand out, each of which involves one of the myriad forms of trade in services.

Fostering trade that helps the transition
Our first area of trade-expansive activity concerns the better exploitation of trade in electricity. Today only some 4 per cent of electricity in wealthy nations is traded across borders, compared with 24 per cent of global gas and 46 per cent of oil. Subsea grids have to be part of the answer – in effect, separating power production from consumption in space, rather than in time, through the currently impracticable use of giant batteries or other forms of storage. To make progress in subsea electricity grids, however, requires further development, and sharing, of the complex engineering services required to relay electricity deep under the ocean. As an example of what can be done, Singapore and Malaysia are cooperating in an exciting project that will see a hydropower project in Borneo, run by Sarawak Energy, export power to Singapore by submarine cable.

Gordon Hanson and Matthew Slaughter (2023) have come up with the constructive idea that the USMCA should facilitate trade in electricity between the signatories by developing the under-exploited potential for hydropower in the Canadian provinces of Quebec and British Columbia.

A second area of environmental opportunity via expanded trade, broadly defined, entails preserving forests through financial transfers. Payments to developing countries, under the Forest Pledge coming out of COP 26 in Glasgow in November 2021, enabling them to reduce deforestation would constitute a valuable form of trade in environmental services. Deforestation is the source of 11 per cent of global carbon dioxide emissions, with some 10 million hectares of forest lost worldwide every year.

Thirdly, scope – and need – exists to foster investment and trade in critical minerals. The IEA estimates that scaling up green tech to meet the Paris Agreement goals will increase demand for lithium, graphite, cobalt and nickel by, respectively, forty-two, twenty-five, twenty-one and nineteen times between 2020 and 2040. Overall, for the most critical raw materials, more than 80 per cent is concentrated in only three countries, with particularly severe export restrictions affecting platinum, germanium, cobalt, bismuth and palladium.[24] There is even talk in Argentina of creating a Lithium OPEC with Bolivia and Chile. To meet the rising demand for these critical minerals requires, again, the expanded trade in engineering services, particularly destined for developing countries, in order to unleash potential supply.

Financial transfers to developing countries also have an important role to play in the wider exploitation of critical minerals, though care will be needed to avoid unintended consequences. A case in point is the agreement reached at COP 27 at Sharm el-Sheikh in November 2022 through which the United States, Japan and others will loan Indonesia $20 billion under a Just Energy Transition Partnership, or JET-P. The money will likely fund 'downstream' ambitions to use Indonesian nickel in battery factories and other high-technology plant, thus helping underpin Jakarta's – questionable – ban on nickel exports and an industry policy that may, or may not, correspond to Indonesia's underlying comparative advantage.

The fourth area of trade-expansive opportunity in the field of services involves cooperation with China. It is important to ensure that the ongoing US–China tech war and the ill-advised pursuit of selective decoupling does not bring further collateral damage to vital cooperation with China on renewable energy. One highly effective transmission mechanism involved here has been the export, by Australia, of education services in electrical engineering to visiting Chinese (and other) students who then use this expertise to develop solar photovoltaic panel manufacturing plants in China for export throughout the world. Looking ahead, as China and other countries move to 'smart energy' policies that depend on digital grids, expertise in information and communications technology and data science will become another increasingly valuable tradable service.

As well as showing the benefit of focusing exports on what you are good at, what this education services case also reminds us is that trade, as well as helping fund the energy transition, has a direct role to play in the pursuit of environmental goals, but as a facilitator, not as a weapon. The same point applies in the field of public health.

The COVID-19 virus and beyond

At the outset, in looking at optimal ways of helping developing countries cope with the COVID-19 virus, its variants and its successors, it needs to be acknowledged that patent relaxation and fostering vaccine production *within* developing countries can only go so far. Pfizer and Moderna have agreed to build factories of their own within developing countries, with early moves in South Africa, Rwanda and Senegal. Johnson & Johnson and Oxford–AstraZeneca have also set up multiple manufacturing sites globally. International institutions are backing these private-sector initiatives with, for example, the International Finance Corporation making significant investments in India, Senegal and South Africa.

In fostering developing country manufacturing capacity, Singapore has been identified as a possible role model. French pharmaceutical company Sanofi's production facility there offers a potential template in digital infrastructure and equipment capabilities that allow for quick changeovers, enabling toggle between three or four different types of vaccine. But here's the rub – and the qualifier to this course of action. Singapore is hardly representative of developing countries, which, for the most part, have neither the trained people nor the regulatory regime needed to establish and maintain a safe and reliable vaccine manufacturing capacity.

Some developing countries also impede their own manufacturing potential by imposing tariffs on critical vaccine inputs. Using the criterion of (at least) a 5 per cent tariff for the product group as a 'choke point', Argentina, India and Iran have choke points in all thirteen product groups of vaccine inputs which can be considered critical (WTO 2021b). In short, new factories will not come online fast enough to meet demand.

So, an intellectual property waiver, in itself, may not have enormous effect in strengthening developing country capabilities. Rigorous testing requirements and complex production methods mean that there are considerable barriers to entry above and beyond intellectual property – barriers to entry which help explain why, globally, there is only one manufacturer of vaccines against Monkey Pox.[25] Moreover, most of the producers with the relevant experience and expertise are already engaged in the production of COVID-19 vaccines. So, an intellectual property waiver may have only limited effect on vaccine availability. Patrick Gaulé (2021) has thus suggested that a more effective way of accelerating vaccine supply is likely to be subsidizing research and development and manufacturing capacity.

This is not to say, however, that nothing can be done on the IPR front. In particular, more can be done, within the WTO, to implement the changes to the TRIPS Agreement intended to improve, more broadly, developing country access to medicines. In 2010, India and Brazil initiated WTO dispute settlement (DS408 and DS409 respectively) arguing that repeated seizures on patent infringement grounds of generic drugs originating in India and transiting the Netherlands on the way to other developing countries were inconsistent with the TRIPS Agreement. Over ten years later, the case remains unresolved.

More could also be done within preferential trade agreements to facilitate developing country access to medicines. The Trans-Pacific Partnership is a case in point. When the United States was actively involved in negotiations it sought a twelve-year period of data exclusivity for biologics – biologically derived drugs, some of which are used in COVID therapy. Even with the US departure, the CPTPP still provides (Article 18.51) for up to eight years of data exclusivity protection for biologics, in what is seen by many health authorities as a deterrent to research and a source of increased public spending on medicines.

But the immediate – and continuing – need is to remove trade impediments and to foster increased dedicated production and export from advanced economies (and developing countries such as India with the necessary capacity) to developing countries of variant-adapted vaccines – whether mRNA, viral vector or recombinant protein vaccines – backed by financial transfers to the poorest countries to enable them to import vaccines. Increasing the production of vaccines may also be the only effective way of tackling vaccine nationalism, such as export curbs. Research by Simon Evenett and his colleagues shows that setbacks in vaccine production in 2021 revealed the concentration of vaccine manufacture in a small club of producer nations, limiting the opportunity to counter vaccine nationalism. The more approved vaccines that are safely produced, the smaller will be the temptation to succumb to zero-sum vaccine nationalism (Evenett et al. 2021).

A persisting need in fostering global vaccine production is thus to seek to ensure the free flow of necessary inputs within the supply chain. In April 2021, WTO Director General Ngozi Okonjo-Iweala met with government and industry representatives to discuss ways of strengthening supply chains.

On a more ambitious level – focusing on facilitating cooperation rather than just avoiding restrictions – there is continuing scope to build on the Trade and Health Initiative introduced by a group of WTO members in late 2020, offering an internationally coordinated programme of fragmented, subsidized production of vaccine components. Scope also exists for cooperation between US authorities and the EU's European Health Emergency Preparedness and Response Authority to set global targets for developing and distributing vaccines, therapeutics and diagnostics that different regions need.

Increased vaccine supply to poorer countries, though essential, is not sufficient, however. It needs to be accompanied by improved vaccine advocacy and, critically, by wider curative treatment in developing countries, such as Pfizer's antiviral pill, because, realistically, many of the poorest countries will not be able to maintain a full repeat vaccination programme. A necessary complement to increased vaccine availability via trade in poorer countries is the establishment of reliable drug distribution channels, making treatment cheap, widely available and free of counterfeits.

All this serves to highlight the need for a holistic approach based on multilateral cooperation to what is likely to be a continuing global challenge. Use of the trade weapon – in restricting developing country access to vaccines, vaccine components and vaccine knowledge – is a self-defeating strategy. To be fully effective, however, action on the trade front will need to be accompanied by public health reform within developing countries. The impact of the COVID pandemic in India, for example, has been accentuated by decades of underinvestment in public health infrastructure, dramatically demonstrated by the shortage of personnel, beds and oxygen. As always, trade cannot do it all.

Closing thoughts and the last word to Jan Tinbergen

Support expressed throughout this chapter for positive, trade-liberalizing action is not to totally rule out restrictive measures in support of the environment and public health. As we have seen – and as many readers will be fully aware – WTO rules, and those of preferential trade agreements modelled on the WTO, do, under GATT Article XX, allow trade restrictive measures to protect human, animal and plant life. To be fully effective, however, action under this article will need a revitalized WTO with a fully functioning dispute settlement mechanism to deal with the litigation that will inevitably ensue. Moreover, some essential criteria need to be met when using this particular provision.

There may be a legitimate case for restricting trade in the interests of public health or the environment. But conditions apply: the threat to health or the environment should be intrinsic to the traded product or service (such as trade in dangerous chemicals or waste); the threat should be measurable and scientifically based (not simply relying on a vague notion of 'precaution'); and the action taken should be non-discriminatory as between countries. As we saw in the discussion of CBAM, there may also be important requirements in terms of the compatibility of the use of Article XX with other international agreements.

Apart from in these closely defined circumstances, where all the necessary criteria are met, weaponizing trade to promote environment or public health objectives should be eschewed.

The work of the Dutch economist Jan Tinbergen offers a principle for avoiding the weaponization of trade in pursuit of non-trade objectives: multiple goals require multiple tools; for policy to work there must be as many independent effective instruments as there are feasible targets.[26] Rather than use the trade weapon as a blunt instrument, it is better to tackle environmental and public health goals directly – backed by trade measures that liberalize rather than restrict.

5

Arms Control: Restraining the Use of the Trade Weapon

The trade weapon – with its long shadow of protectionist capture – will never be totally disarmed. And America and China will continue to be among the principal combatants. China, the principal target of trade weaponry, is likely, as its economy slows and its population ages, to become a more, not less tendentious economic partner, with a leader whose world view is based on the assumption of tension and conflict – an assumption that risks being borne out by the bipartisan view in the US Congress of US–China relations as no less than an existential struggle. Policy makers nevertheless have tools at their disposal to lessen the damaging effects of weaponizing trade while at the same time addressing the underlying tensions between trading nations.

This chapter will draw together from the earlier discussion the opportunities for damage control, and avoidance, under the different uses of the trade weapon and hence for weakening the synergies between those uses. But a key concern here will be to look at ways of addressing the discontents of the liberal trading order that fuel the underlying motivations to co-opt the trade weapon in the service of other goals, whether to punish aggression, pursue self-reliance and national sovereignty, or advance public health or environmental objectives.

The trade weapon will never be totally disarmed

In the fight against aggression – whether across or within borders – there will always be popular support within sender countries for the use of economic sanctions, of which trade measures will form a major part. And, in response to those sanctions, the target will always seek ways of spreading the pain – through counter-sanctions – as Vladimir Putin has done in the course of the war in Ukraine.

Countries will also continue to invoke special circumstances when breaching undertakings they have made – for example, when applying penalty tariffs above the bound rates to which they committed. Moreover, as we have seen, trade rules, as embodied in the GATT, are themselves quite permissive and open to abuse. Ultimately, targeted interference with imports and exports can be invoked – with varying degrees of plausibility – on the basis of extremely broad criteria, whether considered 'necessary to protect human, animal or plant life or health' (GATT Article XX) or 'necessary for the protection of [a WTO member's] essential security interests' (Article XXI).

The cumulative effect of weaponizing trade is a pronounced brake on the free flow of goods and services between countries, putting at risk three decades of gains to growth and income driven by the globalization of production. Fortunately, policy makers are not helpless. As we have seen in preceding chapters, there is plenty of scope to limit and avoid the damage from using the trade weapon.

Pursuing alternatives to use of the trade weapon

In the rather special case of sanctions – which will always be used despite their costs and relative inefficacity – carrots can nevertheless accompany the stick. Complementary action in the form of classic diplomacy can be taken in order to reduce conflict expectations and so increase the chances that current sanctions will work expeditiously and – crucially – that future sanctions might become less necessary. Providing a guarantee of Ukraine's neutrality, together with assurances about its territorial integrity, is likely to be key in curbing Russian aggression on its western border. Providing aid and technical assistance to North Korea will be a necessary counterpart to economic sanctions (and, eventually, sanctions relief) to relieve nuclear tensions on the Korean peninsula.

In all other uses of the trade weapon that we have looked at there are preferable alternatives available:

- promoting resilience within the global value chain as opposed to seeking autonomy through ill-advised re-shoring and friend-shoring.[1] Germany has generated such resilience by developing its liquefied natural gas import facility at Wilhelmshaven to bring greater flexibility to its energy sector;
- promoting rules-based multilateral as opposed to sovereignty-seeking unilateral trade remedies, while applying trade remedies in an economy-wide setting, considering the interests of consumers as well as producers. Taking this economy-wide view is a key part of the work of the Productivity Commission in Australia;
- promoting direct methods to achieve environmental and public health goals as opposed to relying on trade restrictions as a blunt and ineffective instrument – using trade as a facilitator, not a weapon. Work under way in the WTO to reduce fossil fuel subsidies is an important example of serving the environment by reducing, rather than increasing, damaging distortions to trade.

And, by restraining each of the individual uses of the trade weapon, policy makers also have the power to weaken the synergies between them.

But to limit effectively the damage from use of the trade weapon, it will be necessary to address systemic concerns about the WTO – as custodian of the liberal order – and, more broadly, the discontents with the liberal order itself that make the unilateral and opportunistic co-option and subordination of trade policy possible in the first place.

Restoring trust in the trading order: addressing the discontents

Restoring trust in the trading system calls for action on five fronts: improving the help given to those who lose from market opening; bolstering the capacity of economies to adjust to the challenge of international competition; strengthening the advocacy of open markets; reinvigorating multilateral cooperation in trade; and better exploiting the complementary role of regional initiatives. Among these five approaches, arguably the most compelling is that of helping the losers from market opening.

Helping those who lose

Strengthening public acceptance of the case for open markets calls for more than simply demonstrating the gains from liberalization. It also needs acknowledgement that – as we have seen – there are losers as well as winners from market opening, that support will be given to those who lose, and that such support, as pointed out by Jagdish Bhagwati (1988), will be less costly than the protectionist alternative. Such support should – in principle – rely on economy-wide action in order to treat individuals in similar circumstances equally, to provide help to those in genuine need, and to avoid compounding distortions in the economy. In practice, however, experience suggests that successful episodes of trade-related structural adjustment have almost always involved some measure of sector-specific assistance. Given the concentrated costs of liberalization, targeted assistance may be called for, particularly where structural decline in a particular sector causes geographically concentrated job loss beyond what existing labour market programmes can cope with. Put simply, there will be occasions when help has to be tailored to needs.

Should governments then consider it necessary to target assistance in particular cases, experience suggests that problems of both equity and efficiency will be minimized to the extent that such assistance is time-bound, with a clear exit strategy; decoupled from production with incentives to adjust and innovate; aimed at re-employing displaced workers; compatible with general safety-net arrangements; and transparent and accountable. As experience in Scandinavia has shown, if there is a fisheries glut, it is better to help fishers to diversify than to subsidize a new boat.

The United States Trade Adjustment Assistance (TAA) legislation, though not without controversy because of the equity considerations arising, has nevertheless been the source of innovative practices related to the provision of earnings-replacement benefits, such as the wage insurance programme introduced in 2003. It has, however, far from dispelled public concern about trade liberalization. Moreover, a study by David Autor, David Dorn and Gordon Hanson finds that most trade-displaced workers end up relying on social security and disability benefits, rather than the retraining resources provided by TAA (Autor et al. 2016a).[2] This points to the need for a broader, economy-wide approach to trade-related structural adjustment.

Adjusting to trade shocks and technological change

The gains from trade will only be fully realized – and appreciated – in an economy that allows workers and capital to move from declining to expanding areas of activity. This means having macroeconomic policies that promote stability and growth. It means having a sound regulatory framework. This is perhaps one of the key lessons we learned from the 2008–9 global financial crisis: liberalization is not the same as deregulation, and in some areas, such as financial services, increased competition needs to be accompanied by more, not less regulation; this will be a recurring theme of this chapter. And it means having labour market flexibility. Unemployment benefit schemes should provide adequate income support but also promote work incentives. Employment protection should not hamper firms' ability to adjust and workers' incentive to change employer. Wage-setting systems need to be flexible. Housing and pension-portability policies should not hamper regional mobility. And education and training should be geared to meet evolving needs in the labour market.

A case may be made that each one of these measures should be done first: macroeconomic reform to create an enabling environment; regulatory reform through competition policy to promote market contestability and firm entry; labour market reform to promote worker mobility. In practice, governments should try to introduce reforms in parallel so that the synergies between them are fully exploited.[3]

Successful adjustment need not involve radical diversification of economic activity and the abandonment of traditional strengths. The city of Detroit, which was declared bankrupt in 2013 and now has finances in surplus, seems to be bouncing back on the strength of motor vehicle manufacture, with General Motors converting an old plant into an assembly centre for electric vehicles; Stellantis (formerly Fiat–Chrysler) opening a new factory to build Jeep SUVs; and Ford rebuilding Michigan Central Station as a campus for its design teams.[4]

Gladstone in northeastern Australia is, as pointed out by Ross Garnaut,[5] successfully adapting to being at a transmission node for declining fossil-fuel power generation. It is building new trading strengths based on enduring industrial traditions together with established energy, port and training infrastructure. The focus now is on the export of liquefied natural gas and the promise of exportable hydrogen for the cars and power stations of Japan and Korea.

It is not a coincidence of course that the industrial adjustments taking place in locations as different as Detroit and Gladstone are each occurring as part of the shocks, and opportunities, inherent in the energy transition. Another example of building on traditional strengths, while seeking to ensure that education and training are geared to evolving needs, comes from Sheffield in northern England, where the Advanced Manufacturing Research Centre draws together the teaching and research capacities of the University of Sheffield in partnership with industrial leaders Boeing, Rolls Royce and McLaren.[6] A common feature of these well-documented cases of industrial adjustment is the strong if not exclusive focus on the role of exports. In seeking to strengthen public support for open markets, it is just as important, however, to put the case for imports.

Strengthening the advocacy of open markets

The importance of effective and widespread advocacy of openness in getting good outcomes in trade policy – and in fostering informed public support for open markets – cannot be overstated. One important aspect of putting the case for open markets (as just touched on in relation to the global financial crisis) is to dispel a common misunderstanding that freer markets mean less regulation. The tough stance taken by competition authorities in Europe, and increasingly in the United States, against Google is evidence of the importance of the regulatory framework (see box 6)

Box 6 Freer trade does not mean deregulation: US and EU treatment of Google

In September 2022, the EU fined Google's parent company Alphabet €4.12 billion for unlawful restrictions on manufacturers of Android mobile devices and mobile network operators to consolidate the dominant position of its search engine. Earlier, in June 2017, the European Commission announced a €2.42 billion fine against Google for anti-competitive behaviour, concluding it had abused its dominant position as a search engine by giving illegal advantage to its own comparison-shopping service and so making significant gains in traffic at the expense of its rivals and to the detriment of European consumers.

Market dominance, as such, is not illegal under EU antitrust rules. However, dominant firms are considered, under EU law, to have a special responsibility not to abuse their powerful market position by restricting competition, either in the market where they are dominant or in separate markets. Critics, particularly in the United States, accuse the EU of bias against US companies: in August 2016, EU antitrust officials ordered Apple to pay Ireland up to $14.5 billion in taxes, and in May 2017 the Commission fined Facebook $122 million for providing regulators with misleading statements during its acquisition of the messaging service WhatsApp.

What the EU action highlights, however, is not so much a tendency to bias as the basic difference between a US approach to antitrust and abuse of dominance that has tended to be relatively accommodating (even among Democrats, traditionally more interventionist) and a European approach which has been more active in seeking to rein in anti-competitive practice. The charge of bias on the part of the EU must also be considered in light of the fact that the Commission's action against anti-competitive behaviour has recently been targeted at European firms: Daimler (€1 billion), DAF (€753 million), Renault (€670 million) and Iveco (€495 million). The question that does arise, however, is whether the EU policy of fines is effective. The 2022 fine of €4.12 billion represents only 3 per cent of Google's net cash balance and may well be regarded simply as the price of doing business.

Competition law and policy are not set in stone, and change is possible, on both sides of the Atlantic. The EU may have marked a shift in allowing a merger between Alstom and Siemens. And, in the United States, the relatively benign view of Google may be changing. In October 2020, the Department of Justice, together with eleven state attorneys general, filed an antitrust lawsuit against Google for anti-competitive practices in the search market.

Nevertheless, whatever the changes afoot, in both US and EU jurisdictions there is a shared understanding that allowing market forces to work is not the same as a regulatory free for all.

So, pursuing open markets does not mean allowing open slather in regulation. After all, even Friedrich Hayek, one of the most uncompromising advocates of the liberal order, acknowledged the importance of regulation: 'in order that competition should work beneficially, a carefully thought-out legal framework is required' (Hayek 1944: 27). There is now, however, an international consensus that, in the digital age, general regulatory provisions are frequently inadequate and that tailored regulatory regimes are needed as an accompaniment to market opening.[7]

The prime responsibility for putting the case for openness rests with government. But without a wider voice this will be a hard sell. There is also an important role for the academic community and business leaders. But, above all, there is a need for an independent statutory authority to undertake informed and dispassionate analysis of the opportunities and costs of international competition and a responsible media to give that analysis a wider audience.

A good example of the benefit of having a range of voices in the trade debate is provided by the successful reform agenda of the Hawke–Keating governments in Australia in the 1980s, when farm-lobby resistance to market opening was effectively dismantled by a combination of academic, governmental and media analysis and exposure.

During the 1980s, the Australian Labor Party governments of Bob Hawke and Paul Keating extensively liberalized Australian trade policy. In the highly protected motor vehicle and textiles and clothing sectors, import quotas were removed and tariffs reduced, fostering increased innovation, higher productivity and improved export performance.[8] This achievement contrasts with that of an earlier Labor government under Gough Whitlam that also introduced major reform but, in the end, fell short. Whitlam's ambitious, commendable, across the board 25 per cent tariff cut in 1973 was soon selectively reversed with protective quotas.

The contrasting experience of these two governments had many causes, not least the differing scope of the overall reform agenda (Heydon 2020). But it owed much to the role of the farm lobby. Under Whitlam's tenure, Australian farmers successfully advocated the protection of Australian manufacturing as unspent negotiating coin to induce – it was hoped – trading partners to reduce their levels of agricultural protection.[9] Crucially, by the time of Hawke–Keating's tenure, the farm lobby had abandoned this protectionist stance. And that shift was due largely to the successful advocacy of open markets by the Industries Assistance Commission (IAC), an independent statutory authority – and that is important – created by Whitlam to provide impartial procedures for public enquiry and recommendations to government. A senior figure in the National Farmers' Federation in the late 1970s, David Trebeck, is on record as saying that 'the catalytic role played by the IAC during the 1970s in lifting the economic debate and explaining the impact of protection cannot be overstated. We fired the bullets made by the IAC.'[10]

A key part of IAC advocacy was to show that the effective rate of protection[11] for farming was 6 per cent while that for manufacturing was a whopping 28 per cent. It was this as much as anything that led Australian farmers – particularly graziers – to see the folly of using protection as unspent negotiating coin. But, critically, the IAC 'bullets' hit the mark because the protection target had been better exposed by a range of other 'advocates': the academic community, notably Max Corden, providing a robust critique of the cost of protection; advisers close to Hawke and Keating, such as Ross Garnaut, exposing this analysis; and the media, particularly the *Australian Financial Review*, communicating the case for open markets to a wider public. Former *Financial Review* editor Maximilian Walsh, though pumping his own profession, was right in saying that 'you cannot do reform without the media' (cited in Kelly 2016). All this said, the central role in advocating the case for the liberalization of trade and in effecting a turning point in the protection debate was clearly played by the IAC – a Whitlam innovation that, as Gary Banks (2022) has demonstrated, helped lay the foundations for the Hawke–Keating reforms a decade later.

A counterfactual to the example of successful advocacy of trade reform in Australia in the 1980s is the failure of advocacy during the Brexit campaign in the UK in 2016 – where, as part of our story, Brexit can be seen as the weaponization of trade, through reimposed trade restrictions in the name of other goals, including the defence of the Anglosphere. There were many factors other than trade that drove the Brexit debate. But trade played a central role, notably in the claim of the Vote Leave supporters that it would be possible to improve the UK's position, relative to the status quo, by negotiating a free trade agreement with the EU, together with a series of other, welfare-enhancing, trade agreements with countries outside the EU.

There was no shortage of analysis contradicting this claim, but it was either not used effectively or it came out too late. For example, work by Monique Ebell and James Warren showed that downgrading from a single market to a free trade agreement (FTA) with the EU would reduce UK trade by some 20 per cent, while FTAs with the five BRICS countries plus the US, Canada, Australia, New Zealand and Indonesia combined would increase trade by just 5 per cent[12] (Ebell and Warren 2016). This analysis was available ahead of the 23 June 2016 vote but failed to hit the headlines. Two years after the vote, the UK government's own analysis belatedly supported a negative assessment, finding that new FTAs add only 0.2 per cent to UK GDP (UK Government 2018).

The experience with Brexit in 2016 highlights the challenge facing trade advocacy. Econometric modelling of preferential trade agreements is pretty dry stuff compared with the colourful campaigning that helped carry the day for the Leavers. The challenge to open-trade advocacy, in the face of often entrenched vested interests, is now compounded by a series of more recent developments: the growth of a new form of popular sovereignty (when, in 2019, Parliament threatened to stymie Prime Minister Boris Johnson's Brexit plans, he prorogued it in the name of the people); a steady retreat in press freedom around the world (UNESCO 2022); declining public trust in newspaper and television news (at its lowest ever level according to a Gallup survey in the United States in 2022); the growing risk of misinformation, or disinformation, on social media; and the replacement of the traditional left–right configuration of political allegiance with a potentially more strident patriot–globalist confrontation.

In some countries, these recent developments combine with an enduring tendency to resist change. Such an apparent resistance is a recurring theme captured by French social scientists, from Alexis de Tocqueville in the mid-nineteenth century to Alain Peyrefitte in the 1970s and Alain Duhamel today. And with resistance to change comes the need to be protected that readily translates into protection from foreign competition.[13]

Moreover, people's perception of the gains from trade will suffer if they lose trust in their trade partner. According to Lowy Institute polling, in 2022, 63 per cent of Australians considered China (by far Australia's most important two-way trading link) to be more of a security threat to Australia than an economic partner, up from 12 per cent in 2018. As at the end of 2022, almost 90 per cent of Japanese had a negative view of China – again the main trading partner – up from 71 per cent a year earlier. This perception does, however, seem to vary with the age of the respondent. Polling by *The Economist* and YouGov shows a striking difference in Americans' views of China by age. Some 25 per cent of those aged eighteen to forty-four view China as an enemy compared with some 52 per cent of those aged forty-five and over.[14]

Together, these factors form a high hurdle in the path to better advocacy, though not an insurmountable one, particularly when the media can be enlisted in support. This challenge to advocacy will need to be confronted in fostering support for the next of our steps in restraining the motivation to use the trade weapon: reinvigorating multilateral cooperation in trade.

Reviving the WTO[15]

World Trade Organization Director-General Ngozi Okonjo-Iweala said the measures agreed upon at the twelfth WTO Ministerial Conference (MC12) on 12 June 2022 'will make a difference to the lives of people around the world.' She may be right on some specifics, but turning the MC12 into a game-changer for the trading order will require a level of political resolve from G20 leaders that so far is sadly lacking. Five outcomes from the WTO ministerial stand out.

1. After twenty years of negotiation, an agreement to end harmful fisheries subsidies was reached. This included the absolute prohibition of subsidies for fishing in the high seas. In its twenty-seven-year history, this is only the second multilateral agreement on new trade rules agreed upon by the WTO.
2. A waiver was signed under the Agreement on Trade-Related Aspects of Intellectual Property Rights (TRIPS). As we have seen, it allows for the manufacture and export of COVID-19 vaccines without the consent of the patent holder. And it does so in a way that differentiates between developing countries – a longstanding problem within the WTO.[16]
3. Despite fears from the business sector that the moratorium on customs duties on e-commerce would end, an agreement was reached to extend the moratorium until the next ministerial conference.
4. In response to the acute food situation, members agreed to exercise restraint on implementing export restrictions and to exempt World Food Programme humanitarian purchases from such restrictions.
5. And members also committed to work towards WTO reform – including the goal of creating a fully functioning dispute settlement mechanism no later than 2024.

One might quibble. Even if there is full implementation, fisheries subsidies are only one part of the environmental challenge. The WTO still needs to liberalize trade in environmental goods and services and impose discipline on fossil fuel subsidies. As for the COVID-19 vaccine initiative, it will not provide developing countries with the technical capacity needed to actually produce vaccines. (Both these points came up in chapter 4.) In e-commerce, critical questions remain about the right balance between data access and data protection. And 'exercising restraint' on food export restrictions still leaves scope for abuse.

But, despite their shortcomings, the measures announced at MC12 are all steps in the right direction. Moreover, they are being backed by ongoing cooperative activities within the WTO. One of these is the negotiation among participating WTO members on e-commerce and – indeed – issues such as data protection. This brings together key players, including the United States and China, in a plurilateral agreement that does not require the elusive goal of compliance by all WTO members. It may offer a welcome, if small, area of cooperation between Washington and Beijing. The plurilateral talks on electronic commerce constitute what is known in the WTO as a Joint Statement Initiative (JSI). Other JSIs cover investment facilitation for development, services domestic regulations, micro, small and medium-sized enterprises, and environmental sustainability.

But the positive steps described here cannot disguise the fact that there is a systemic challenge to the liberal order of which the WTO is part, as the trading system becomes increasingly exposed to the twin temptations of self-reliance and unbridled national sovereignty in trade defence. Whether the achievements of the MC12 represent a new beginning for the WTO is still an open question.

Seeking to answer that question brings us back to the fifth and arguably most important of the MC12 measures – restoring a fully functioning dispute settlement mechanism. As we saw briefly in chapter 3, the dispute settlement mechanism has been disabled since December 2019 by a US blockage of the appointment of Appellate Body judges in response to what Washington sees as judicial overreach and bias against trade remedies on the part of the Appellate Body. The provisional Multiparty Interim Appeal Arbitration Arrangement, with its incomplete membership, is not a viable long-term solution.

Effective dispute settlement is critically important for two reasons: because of the need to defuse trade disputation and because of the synergies between the WTO's judicial and legislative functions. As Bernard Hoekman (2022) has pointed out, progress on the judicial front is critical in enhancing the (legislative) prospects of concluding negotiations on longstanding subjects such as agricultural policies, which proved impossible at MC12, and matters not even tabled at MC12, including rules on the use of trade policy in combating climate change, managing competitive spillovers of industrial subsidies, and regulating production processes and supply chains.

In the broadest terms, restoring a comprehensive WTO dispute settlement mechanism calls for a rediscovery of the balance between acceptance of the rules of the liberal world order, enshrined in the WTO, and the exercise of national sovereignty by WTO members – what Francis Fukuyama calls the difficult but necessary marriage of national identity and liberal universalism.[17] What this means in practical terms is addressing the particular US discontent about a perceived WTO bias against the use of trade remedies. And at least part of the answer to that is, as we have seen, the need to clarify the status – and treatment – of state-owned enterprises. It might also help to de-politicize the dispute settlement process by introducing a periodic review mechanism for panel and Appellate Body decisions, where members could discuss and clarify their respective positions.[18]

Without full restoration of WTO dispute settlement, it will be extremely difficult to restrain the use of the trade weapon – whether by unilaterally breaching bound tariffs or by unjustifiably invoking GATT Articles XX and XXI – and, particularly, to defuse the trade sovereignty concerns discussed in chapter 3. The prime responsibility for advancing these different items on the WTO agenda lies with the leaders and trade officials of the G20 nations – the world's most powerful economies. Collectively, the G20 as an institutional force could usefully stress that self-reliance and unilateralism are simply a recipe for protectionist capture, retaliation and trade friction.

More specifically, there are three areas where, building on the momentum of MC12, useful synergies could be developed between the G20 process and the work of the WTO, leading to soft law recommendations on best practice.

The first would be to marry the analytical tools and policy-monitoring activities of the WTO (together with those of the World Bank, UNCTAD and the OECD) with the G20 leaders' meetings to explore practical opportunities to address WTO members' concerns about supply-chain vulnerability and the associated push to self-reliance. A precedent for this was set at the September 2013 G20 leaders' summit in St Petersburg (in happier times), when participants discussed a joint study prepared by the OECD, WTO and UNCTAD on *Implications of Global Value Chains for Trade, Investment, Development and Jobs*.

One focus for discussion could be the need for improved disciplines in the provision of subsidies and grants to sectors, firms and workers to help them cope with supply-chain shocks. This would cover a number of things: establishing greater clarity in identifying the ultimate beneficiary of support within complex supply chains, determining whether existing trade rules cover all the support provided by government-invested firms (state-owned enterprises) and evaluating the scope of hard to measure support through the financial system via below-market loans and government equity injections (OECD 2021b).

Another supply-chain focus could be on cooperation on emergency preparedness and management in the framework of the WTO Agreement on Government Procurement. And, more broadly, scope also exists for multilateral discussion and cooperation to share information, of which no single government is likely to have possession, on concentration and bottlenecks in the global value chain and the establishment of stress tests for essential supply chains (Hoekman et al. 2021).

A second area of potential linkage between the G20 process and the work of the WTO is to explore the possibilities for more extensive analytical support by the WTO Secretariat for developing countries engaged – or often not engaged – in plurilateral negotiations among interested parties. And the third area of potential synergies involving the G20 – admittedly, highly sensitive and complex – is to examine, on an informal basis in selected cases, possible opportunities (as

Arms Control 155

outlined in chapter 1) to marry the trade sanctions stick with the classic diplomacy carrot.

Realistically, G20 engagement will be incremental and at the lowest common denominator. The leaders' declaration from the Bali G20 summit in November 2022 is strong on broad exhortations but light on specifics. And where particular reform issues are addressed, the time horizon is deliberately vague – no doubt the product of tortuous negotiation: for attainment of global net zero greenhouse gas emissions/carbon neutrality 'by or around mid-century'; for fossil fuel subsidy reform 'over the medium term'; and, for action on the WTO dispute settlement mechanism, the commitment is only to 'discussions ... on the path leading to MC13'. In some cases, there is no timeline, as with the commitment 'to reinforce international trade and investment cooperation to address supply-chain issues and avoid trade disruptions.'

Ultimately, progress within the G20 will depend on the trading majors. And, though a liberal reawakening in Washington and Beijing seems highly remote, the groundwork for their engagement, and that of the G20, in restraining the weaponization of trade has nevertheless been laid by the twelfth WTO Ministerial Conference. It will now be for the emerging economies to carry the G20 torch, with India, Brazil and South Africa serving, respectively, as chairs in 2023, 2024 and 2025. How might these multilateral efforts be complemented by cooperation at the regional level?

Acting regionally

Given the geostrategic tensions between Washington and Beijing, the growing economic clout of China and the ambivalence of many Asian countries about their economic dependence on China, it is not surprising that the Asia-Pacific region is a key theatre in the engagement of the trade weapon. Fortunately, within the Asia-Pacific, a network of cooperative bodies offers opportunities for collective trade reform and for engagement, in particular, with China.

Beijing has expressed an interest in becoming a member of the Comprehensive and Progressive Agreement for

Trans-Pacific Partnership (CPTPP). As Peter Drysdale and Shiro Armstrong have rightly stressed, if China can demonstrate a commitment to the high standard rules – written largely by the Bush and Obama administrations before US defection, precisely with China in mind – that would be in the region's interests (Drysdale and Armstrong 2022). Importantly, CPTPP membership would commit China to reform in three crucial areas: to limit subsidies for large SOEs, permit freer cross-border data flows and ban forced labour.

China has in fact committed to trialling CPTPP rules in some of its free trade zones, though it must be acknowledged that part of Beijing's interest in membership is to promulgate its own interpretation of global trade rules. For example, despite China's mixed-ownership reforms of its SOEs, private shareholders remain subordinate to the state. As we saw in chapter 3, a possible basis for agreement on SOEs would be an undertaking from China to end subsidies for SOEs operating in competitive markets abroad, in return for more tolerance for those supplying public services within China.

China's ability to sign on to freer cross-border data flows will be a big ask. A data-protection law passed in August 2021 will in fact make it harder for foreign companies to move data out of China. Here, Beijing seems to be moving in the opposite direction to that required for CPTPP membership. Nevertheless, here too there may be the seeds of a solution were PTA – or indeed WTO – rules on digital standards to ensure that companies such as Huawei cannot be excluded from Western markets simply because they are Chinese, or were there to be wider adoption of the public–private scrutiny of firms such as Huawei that exists in the UK.

The third element of CPTPP eligibility – banning forced labour – is no less tricky, given Beijing's iron fist in Xinjiang, but also not insoluble were (as touched on in chapter 1) outside auditors to be permitted to examine, and in certain cases perhaps give the green light to, selected supply chains.

China is already a member of another regional grouping, the Regional Comprehensive Economic Partnership (RCEP), which has built-in mechanisms to engage ministers and leaders in an agenda of economic cooperation that kicked off in November 2022. Though spurned by America and India, RCEP is a useful forum for ASEAN commitment to trade reform, with an important practical contribution in simplifying rules of origin among the signatories. Moreover, in eleven of the fifteen member states, intra-RCEP imports already account for more than half of total imports – principally because of the presence of China in the agreement.

However, both these bodies (RCEP and CPTPP), being preferential arrangements, are, it must be said, 'second best' to multilateral opening because of the unavoidable fact of trade diversion at the expense of third parties – as we saw in the introduction. One recently established body that does not entail trade diversion is the Biden administration's Indo-Pacific Economic Framework for Prosperity (IPEF), launched in May 2022 and with membership accounting for 40 per cent of global GDP and including Australia, India, Indonesia, Japan and Vietnam. There is no trade diversion because the agreement contains no provisions on trade liberalization. That, together with the deliberate exclusion of China – whose pivotal role in the region cannot simply be wished away by Washington – has prompted fairly widespread criticism of IPEF outside and within the United States.[19]

IPEF has four pillars – Connected Economy, Resilient Economy, Clean Economy and Fair Economy – and does not require congressional approval, signalling that the United States does not intend to make significant concessions. The hope, notably in Japan, that IPEF might pave the way for a US return to the CPTPP would seem a long shot. The Biden administration, fearful of alienating union supporters and a trade-wary public, has not even tried to rebuild a domestic coalition in favour of joining the CPTPP.

Unnamed in the IPEF declaration but of overriding importance are the implicit US security assurances to Asian partners that find themselves at odds with China. And IPEF will address a number of issues that will strike a chord with Asian partners, notably digital trade, competition policy, bribery and accelerated port-clearance times within the supply chain. Given their disparate membership and rules, these three bodies – CPTPP, RCEP and IPEF – will add complexity to Asia-Pacific trade relations. What must be hoped is that they will nevertheless provide useful channels of communication and ideas into the G20 process and, in particular, the work of the G20 Working Group on Trade, Investment and Industry, while also acting as an external stimulus to needed domestic reform within member countries.

The former Indonesian trade minister Mari Pangestu has proposed four areas where action could be advanced by RCEP–G20 attention: improved border procedures; safe digitalized protocols to encourage business and tourism travel; liberalized trade in environmental goods and services; and technical cooperation to help less-developed countries profit from economic integration (Pangestu and Ing 2022). To these issues, might be added a fifth: preferential trade agreements also have a role in helping promote resilience by virtue of the wider scope of policy issues they now address. Preferential agreements have thus evolved from shallow FTAs, dealing with the elimination of duties and other restrictive regulations of commerce, into comprehensive economic cooperation agreements covering policy areas such as competition, foreign direct investment protection, environment and labour.

A number of PTAs have provisions dealing with the need to promote resilience in specific areas. For example, the agreement between the EU and Singapore refers to the responsibility of Singapore's Agri-Food and Veterinary Authority for ensuring a resilient supply of safe food. The agreement between the EU and the UK explicitly requires the parties to cooperate in strengthening cyber resilience and the ability to fight cybercrime effectively. And an increasing number of preferential agreements also include provisions seeking to promote resilience to climate change – for example, the agreements between the Eurasian Economic Union and Singapore, between China and Mauritius, between Brazil and Chile, and between the EU and Georgia.

More broadly, it has been suggested that, as normative models, PTAs might be seen as paving the way for more international cooperation on economic resilience (WTO 2021d). The fact remains, however, that the primary responsibility for promoting economic resilience rests with the policies of economic management executed at the national level. In coming years these policies are going to be severely put to the test.

Trade peace for our time?

On some counts, it might be postulated that there will be an easing of the commercial tensions between America and China under which many of the trade weapon campaigns are being waged. China is not the Soviet Union and does not seek to overthrow capitalism. Moreover, China might be seen as less threatening as reform momentum slows and it becomes more inward-looking, with no more 'big in, big out'; less attractive to foreign firms, with Apple shifting iPhone production to India; older, with a fertility rate of 1.3 children per woman, well below the 2.1 needed to keep a population stable; and less dynamic, with productivity stagnating after showing impressive growth in the 2000s.[20]

However, the reading that a less dynamic China will be a more compliant partner is wrong on two counts. China will remain a major power, posing an increasingly important challenge to US technological leadership. The data also need to be seen in perspective: as American and other Western companies move out of China, with its rising wage costs, into countries such as Vietnam and Thailand, Chinese firms will often accompany them; China's demographically older population is also a lot smarter; and productivity growth has also been falling in America. But most importantly, under Xi Jinping, China will continue to see the world in combative terms and without a major commitment to reform (see box 7). A less dynamic China will be a potentially more tendentious and difficult interlocutor and trading partner, albeit a vitally important one.

Box 7 The thoughts of Chairman Xi at the Twentieth Congress and what might have been

Whatever he himself actually thinks, Xi Jinping, in his report to the twentieth Communist Party Congress in October 2022, clearly wishes the people of China to see an international environment that is both threatening and dangerous.[21] He calls for resistance to foreign powers 'bent on containing China', speaks of 'drastic changes in the international landscape, especially external attempts to blackmail, contain, blockade and exert maximum pressure on China', and calls for 'a fighting spirit and a firm determination to never yield to coercive power'. There is no reference as there was in his nineteenth Party Congress address to 'countries ... becoming increasingly interconnected and interdependent'.

The policy lessons drawn by Xi are correspondingly uncompromising and essentially inward looking, exhorting Communist Party members to seize strategic opportunities in a shifting international balance of power (code for US decline), placing a high priority on self-reliance in a hostile world, and offering self-congratulation in effectively containing 'ethnic separatists, religious extremists and violent terrorists'. Perhaps most telling, and most discouraging, is the absence from Xi Jinping's report of any reference to *zhengzhi tizhi gaige* (political structural reform) – a principle that has featured in every one of the five-yearly Communist Party Congress reports since it first appeared at the thirteenth congress in 1987.

As a tantalizing hint of 'what might have been', the principle of structural reform, snubbed by Xi, was introduced into the 1987 congress report by the then premier, the liberal Zhao Ziyang. Writing in his diary at the time he was drafting the 1987 report, Zhao expressed support for 'the rejection and correction of the planned economy, the exclusivity of public ownership and the single method of wealth distribution', noting that 'the

> practice of implementing orthodox socialist principles in the style of the Soviet Union was excessive for China's level of socioeconomic development and productivity. This was a leftist mistake' (Zhao 2009: 205). Premier Zhao Ziyang was dethroned and placed under house arrest for attempting to stop the Tiananmen massacre in 1989 and spent the last sixteen years of his life in seclusion.

In short, there is no reason to believe that the forces behind the four campaigns of trade weaponry will diminish.

First, mankind's proclivity to quarrel, both within and across borders, combined with an equally strong human instinct to help the victims of these quarrels, will ensure continuation of costly but largely ineffective trade and other sanctions against aggression. Second, the headwinds that are slowing the globalization of production will not end it, and, precisely because of this, the damaging pursuit of subsidy-fuelled self-reliance in the face of concerns about supply-chain vulnerability will persist. Third, in the perennial struggle between the exercise of national sovereignty and compliance with the international rules of the trading system, the pendulum has definitively shifted towards power-based trade defence in the name of national security, not least in the United States and the European Union. Fourth, protectionist capture and retaliation against trade restrictions and distortions designed to build national capacity to meet environmental and public health objectives will continue to ensure that such measures do more harm than good.

And underpinning each of these forces is the prospect that failure to address the discontents of trade – and a corresponding ascendancy of populism over globalism within the G20 economies – will continue to foster the co-option of the trade weapon for other goals. This tendency is made even likelier by the growing tensions associated with the burgeoning growth of digital trade and associated concerns about cyber security. As at the end of 2022, no less than

70 cyber security-related measures had been notified to the WTO Technical Barriers to Trade Committee (WTO 2022). Here, as elsewhere, there is need for give and take.

China, for its part, must recognize that, if it wants its companies to operate on a global scale in sensitive sectors, adaptations to its autocratic model will be necessary. Take, for example, TikTok, the social media app with over 1 billion users. In order to demonstrate that TikTok is genuinely autonomous, the efforts by ByteDance, its China-based owner, to separate the app's management from its parent company must go further. TikTok should eventually be responsible to a board of its own, with members from outside China and voting rights more broadly distributed. And its algorithms should be available for examination.

For their part, the United States and the European Union must recognize that there are limits to what can be achieved by policies of restriction and reining in the activities of other players. A case in point is the Trade and Technology Council (TTC), a high-level grouping of American and European officials established to foster transatlantic cooperation in the digital world. Some of its activities are quite unexceptionable: helping to advance negotiations on Privacy Shield – an agreement to create a clear legal basis for flows of personal data across the Atlantic – or developing a shared hub of metrics and methodologies for measuring the trustworthiness and risks of artificial intelligence. Freer trade in information technology and digital trade does not mean open slather.[22]

But an increasing focus of TTC activities, especially since Russia's invasion of Ukraine, has been to decide which technology exports to block and which domestic technology developments to favour. As we have seen repeatedly, here there is a serious risk of unintended consequences. Blocking exports is likely simply to accelerate the target's push for self-sufficiency. And picking winners is likely to create disruption where it is least intended.

A particular wish of American officials is to speed up deployment of two new ways of building mobile networks, called OpenRAN (for Open Radio Access Network) and 'virtualization', to provide more competition for Huawei.

The problem is that OpenRAN and virtualization also weaken two large European firms, Ericsson and Nokia, which are in the same business as Huawei. Hence the recourse – referred to frequently in these pages – of simply blocking Huawei's access to essential inputs. The problem is that China – Huawei's country of origin – is central to most tech supply chains and the repository of vast investments by both American and European firms. China, and Chinese firms, will on occasion need to be confronted, and Western cyber security needs to be strengthened. But China needs to be engaged.

Pursuing the case of Huawei, there is here – as always with the trade weapon – a better way of dealing with concerns associated with potentially invasive technology, if it is allowed to work. The UK government in 2010 entered an arrangement with Huawei under which the company's products in the British telecoms market would undergo an annual security evaluation, conducted by the Huawei Cyber Security Evaluation Centre (HCSEC), whose governing board would include a Huawei representative along with senior UK officials from government and the UK telecom sector. If the annual evaluation found areas of concern, it would make them public and state their rationale. And indeed, in 2019, the HCSEC report found that Huawei software posed risks to British operators and *would require significant adjustments*.

However, the eventual decision to ban Huawei from the UK market had less to do with the HCSEC report than with pressure from the US government, which had itself earlier imposed major restrictions on the company. The HCSEC process shows a possible way forward that is transparent and inclusive and better than trade restrictions to starve Huawei of essential inputs at considerable cost to the company and its customers, including the many low-income countries in Africa and elsewhere that use its equipment.[23] There is, however, regrettably, little indication of a willingness to pursue a more constructive course in relation to Huawei, any more than there is in relation to information technology and digital trade more generally.

Digital trade holds the key to global productivity growth in the future. Yet with regional agreements such as the EU digital single market, the North American Digital Trade Zone, the ASEAN E-Commerce Agreement and the continental e-commerce protocols in Africa and Latin America, there is a serious risk of disruptive fragmentation in digital trade. There is also the ever present risk of cyber-attack: the WannaCry ransom ware attributed to North Korea infected more than 200,000 computers across 153 countries, costing hundreds of millions of dollars. But there is also the danger that concerns about cyber security become a catch-all to justify political control or to protect domestic industry from online competitors – with the possibility of invoking the GATT Article XXI national security exception for this purpose.

Such restrictions, including provisions that data be localized, can seriously reduce opportunities – as discussed in chapter 2 – for companies to use big data analytics to assess and manage supply-chain disruption.[24] And there is a danger – as identified by work at ECIPE on the EU Digital Markets Act and Digital Services Act – that new digital regulations, however necessary, will continually reinforce size advantages for big firms – and big economies.[25]

These threats make even more important the cross-cutting work of the WTO plurilateral group on e-commerce that has the added virtue of bringing together America and China as partners rather than adversaries – reminding us that there is a better way than the use of trade weaponry. But that better way will need working for with persistence and conviction: advancing imaginative diplomacy to accompany the use of sanctions; building genuine resilience – and tech inventiveness – within the supply chain on the basis of sound domestic policy and practices; fully restoring trust in the multilateral trade defence tools of the WTO; and attacking environmental and public health goals directly, not via the blunt instrument of trade restriction and distortion.

At stake are three decades of growth built on open markets and the globalization of production. And at risk is the ability to deal successfully with the climate transition and the next pandemic.

Notes

Introduction
1. As we shall see, for most US, and indeed EU, uses of the trade weapon, the main target is China. So why not use that as the organizing principle rather than, as here, splitting up the uses according to different motivations? The reason is that it is important to differentiate specific rationalizations for weaponizing trade because this enables a more targeted discussion of alternatives to use of the trade weapon. The same logic applies when a particular tool, say export restrictions, can be used either as a sanction against aggression or as a way of dealing with supply chain concerns; again, the motivation for use of the weapon will be the organizing principle.
2. The closest approximation might be the bi-directional cascades within a neural network.
3. For a technical discussion of ways of quantifying NTMs, see Berden and Francois (2015).
4. For more on this, see Ferrantino (2012).
5. This move, however, may well prompt foreign suppliers to cease investing within the USMCA region and simply export directly to the United States.
6. This stylized example is drawn from Samuelson (1951).
7. New Trade Theory did not fully explain why only a minority of firms engage in export following market opening. To resolve this question, models were developed that introduced firm-level differences to explain market penetration asymmetries. These 'firm heterogeneity models', also known as New New Trade Theory, explain how trade liberalization leads to uneven innovation responses among firms, reallocating resources to exporting firms with higher productivity and pushing weaker firms out of the market. For more on New Trade Theory,

see Helpman and Krugman (1985), and on New New Trade Theory, Melitz (2003).
8 Respectively, Panagariya (2012), Ranis (1999) and Little (1996).
9 *The Economist* 'Free Exchange' column, 26 February 2022.
10 Since the early 1980s, in the United States, the share of pre-tax income earned by the top 1 per cent has nearly doubled.
11 For more on these differing propositions, see Piketty (2014), Milanović (2016), Kuznets (1953) and Haskel and Westlake (2017).
12 For more on this fundamental point, see Irwin (2002).
13 See Farrell and Newman (2019) and Drezner et al. (2021).

Chapter 1 Sanctioning Aggression
1 See van Bergeijk (2021).
2 *EU-Wide Survey*, 22 June 2022.
3 Speech given in Indianapolis, 4 September 1919.
4 A related point to that of conflict expectations is that made by Agathe Demarais that sanctions unpredictability is an impediment to their effectiveness when targets do not believe that the sender will keep its side of the bargain (Demarais 2022: 256).
5 Quoted in Drezner (1999).
6 Quoted in Baek (1988).
7 United States Office of Technology Assessment, *Nuclear Proliferation and Safeguards*, 1977.
8 *Le Monde*, 11 September 2022.
9 Conversation in *Foreign Affairs* with Sue Mi Terry, 15 December 2022.
10 The challenge in respect of North Korea is compounded by geo-political rivalries. In May 2022, China and Russia vetoed an American-drafted UN resolution tightening sanctions on the DPRK after it tested ballistic missiles.
11 Trita Parsi, Last chance for America and Iran, *Foreign Affairs*, 26 August 2022. See also Maria Fantappie and Vali Nasr, What America should do if Iran nuclear deal talks fail, *Foreign Affairs*, 1 July 2022. The complexity of Western sanctions policy towards Iran was given a new twist in late 2022 with the apparent use by Russia of Iranian delta-winged Shahed-136 drones in Ukraine and, separately, with the brutal repression of public demonstrations by Iranian authorities.
12 Russian propaganda networks pushed the line that Western sanctions, rather than Russia's blockade of the Black Sea, caused the spike in food prices.

13 Early on in the war, Moscow closed some 260 publications. It also blocked Facebook, Instagram and Twitter, accessible only via VPN (virtual private network) proxies, though it was difficult to find a VPN that the authorities had not already also blocked.
14 Daniel Drezner himself finds ambiguous the 'domestic politics' explanation of sanctions effectiveness. He points out rightly that – in the case of the sender – a two-level game approach argues that unanimous domestic support enhances the sender's bargaining position because it reduces the chance of the sender reversing its strategy, while an incomplete information approach would make the opposite claim: that domestic audience costs send an effective signal of resolve to the target country. It nevertheless seems plausible that an autocratic target regime will be better able to withstand the costs of sanctions than a democratically accountable regime.
15 Speech given in Paris, 17 March 2022.
16 *The Economist*, 27 August 2022.
17 *Le Monde*, 24 July 2022.
18 *The Australian*, 28 April 2022.
19 According to media reports in July 2022, this was pure retaliation on Russia's part; the faulty turbine had been repaired in Canada and returned to Germany. It could have been reinstalled at any time.
20 There may of course be some third-party gains from sanctions. For example, the IMF revised up its 2022 growth forecasts for Argentina, Brazil, Colombia and Peru, all prospective beneficiaries of higher energy or cereal prices. Such gains, however, will fan inflationary pressures and hardly ameliorate the overall net disruption.
21 Presciently, Henry Farrell and Abraham Newman (2019) chose the SWIFT network as a case study in their examination of globalized interdependence.
22 Xiao Qiang of the University of California, Berkeley, has estimated that some 10 million Chinese were using VPNs daily during the early stage of the transition out of zero-COVID, up from 2 million at the start of pandemic. Critically, this was the first time that online dissent had coalesced into physical protest.
23 Agathe Demarais (2022) is right that America needs partners in imposing sanctions if target harm is to be maximized. But the history of sanctions, including recent experience with Russia's

invasion of Ukraine, shows that, while partnership is necessary, it is not sufficient to guarantee that sanctions will be effective.
24 In a quantitative analysis of sanctions data, Peter van Bergeijk (2009) finds that more than 40 per cent of successful sanctions require less than one year to achieve their goal. This, however, may simply reflect the fact that sanctions conducive to succeeding will do so relatively quickly.
25 *The Australian*, 1 April 2022.
26 A point made by Nicholas Mulder early on in the Ukraine sanctions case (Mulder 2022a). Classic diplomacy, while possibly helping sanctions to work by encouraging target flexibility, may on occasion (and somewhat paradoxically) obviate the need for sanctions at all – when the carrot is enough.
27 See Pickering (2023).
28 For more on this, see Dale C. Copeland, When trade leads to war: China, Russia and the limits of interdependence, *Foreign Affairs*, 23 August 2022.
29 Freedom House reports that democracy had declined globally for sixteen consecutive years (Gorokhovskaia and Linzer 2022).

Chapter 2 Arming the Global Value Chain
1 Though much of the US subsidy is in the form of tax breaks, an overall tax impost cannot be avoided if there is not to be an unsustainable budget deficit.
2 Readers will see that the discussion in this chapter of supply-chain nervousness, induced, in part, by COVID-19 disruptions, anticipates discussion in chapter 4 of trade and the pandemic. The difference is that this chapter is about disruption caused by COVID-19, while chapter 4 is about the public health dimension of the pandemic itself and the role of trade policy in dealing with it.
3 For more, see Baldwin (2012) and Heydon (2020).
4 See Jones and Kierzkowski (1990), Melitz and Redding (2012) and Antràs and Helpman (2004).
5 The literature also includes the principle of horizontal fragmentation that involves the establishment of production plants in target markets; see, for example, Miroudot (2012).
6 US Department of Commerce data, cited in *Le Monde*, 1 October 2017.
7 See, for example, Carvalho et al. (2020).
8 UNCTAD (2014).
9 See Milanović (2016) and Hausmann (2014).

10 The Biden administration has also barred American investment in a range of Chinese surveillance-tech companies.
11 Hosuk Lee-Makiyama and Robin Baker, The paradox of Washington's 5G sanctions, *East Asia Forum*, 8 August 2022.
12 A government-driven process that may not reflect market realities. Another way of looking at the 'picking winners' problem is to say that, had the country in question a genuine comparative advantage in the product targeted, it would most likely have been producing it anyway.
13 *Financial Times*, 7 February 2023.
14 For example, see OECD (2021a).
15 See Yasuyuki Todo, Japan's post-COVID-19 approach to supply chains, *East Asia Forum*, 3 July 2022.
16 See Anwar (2021).
17 ASEAN-Japan Centre, *Global value chains in ASEAN*, January 2019, www.asean.or.jp/en/centre-wide/centrewide_en/.
18 See González et al. (2019).
19 See Goh (2016).
20 An earlier version of this material appeared under the *East Asia Forum* of the Crawford School of Public Policy at the Australian National University on 10 November 2021.
21 Infant industry policies – pursued since the early nineteenth century, building on the work of Alexander Hamilton and Friedrich List – are invoked in support of time-bound protection to enable learning by doing ('dynamic learning externalities'), correction of market failure, such as insufficient investment, and promotion of eventual gains from economies of scale.
22 It is thus said that policies formerly pursued by countries such as Korea to protect its motor vehicle industry would, in the framework of the GVC, be neither realistic nor sustainable. See Taglioni and Winkler (2016).
23 Writing in the *Australian Financial Review*, 30 April 2020.
24 Based on an interview with BASF chief executive Martin Brudermüller, reported in *The Economist* 'Schumpeter' column, 28 May 2022.
25 See also Baldwin (2022).
26 See Rudd (2022).
27 Herskovic et al. (2020).
28 Alain Garnier, Gaz américain contre data européennes, *Le Monde*, 19 September 2022.
29 See IMF (2022) and Góes and Bekkers (2022).

30 The functioning of the GVC currently depends on disparate 'processing trade' schemes, whereby goods are imported duty free (into the EU, for example) when used for processing prior to their incorporation in exported products. It has been suggested that harmonization of these schemes could yield significant efficiency gains. See Cernat (2022). Nevertheless, the processing schemes, by differentiating among imports according to use, might be seen as themselves adding to complexity, even when harmonized.
31 Xi's report to the Twentieth Communist Party Congress, October 2022.
32 A former Australian ambassador to China, Geoff Raby, has said that basing foreign policy on the premise of conflict is what is to be expected from the dominant power which is being challenged but quite another thing for a country such as Australia, which is not a strategic rival of China and which is utterly dependent on China for its economic wellbeing (Raby 2020).
33 These papers are summarized in the *The Economist* 'Free Exchange' column, 28 May 2022.
34 Industry peak bodies are also likely to support engagement. In 2021, the Association of German Industry (BDI) published a paper, *Responsible Coexistence with Autocracies in Foreign Economic Policy Making*, which concluded that cutting commercial ties with autocracies is not a realistic option.
35 On some of these points, see also Miroudot and Nordstrom (2020).

Chapter 3 Trade Self-Defence

1 To clarify our terminology, self-reliance and self-defence can be seen as two related but distinct expressions of sovereignty (or autonomy): freedom from dependence on others' goods and services and freedom from dependence on others' justice.
2 The international trade lawyers John Jackson and Steve Charnovitz have spoken of 'the constant tension between the claims of authority and allocation of power by nation-state and other WTO members on the one hand, and the assertions of the WTO as an international legitimate authority requiring control of some issues in order to carry out its responsibilities on the other.' As these authors note, this tension is reflected in the vast jurisprudence of the WTO dispute settlement system, offering many lessons about 'classical dilemma situations' (Jackson and Charnovitz 2012).

3 For more on this, see Messerlin and Woolcock (2012).
4 It should be noted that safeguard actions have a much wider coverage in terms of products and countries targeted, so that one safeguard action is often equivalent to many anti-dumping actions. This, however, does not detract from the relative dominance, within the broad body of trade remedies, of anti-dumping action.
5 There is academic work supporting the counter-cyclical interpretation of anti-dumping activity, including that by Meredith Crowley (2011).
6 Historical data show average dumping margins of 15 to 20 per cent when calculations are based on pure price comparisons, 25 per cent when they are based on constructed-value methods, but over 40 per cent in the case of non-market economies (Messerlin 2004; GAO 2006).
7 For more on this, see Puccio (2015) and WTO (2001).
8 US concerns about the perceived threat to national sovereignty arising from dispute settlement extend also to preferential trade agreements. In the 2018 NAFTA review, though Canada succeeded in retaining 'chapter 19' dispute settlement provisions, under the USMCA, dispute settlement will not apply to tariffs levied on national security grounds.
9 An example of coercion was the Chinese threat of tariffs on European cars to pressure Germany into accepting Huawei's bid to build 5G infrastructure in Germany.
10 Francois et al. (2018). Although there is debate about the scale of the impact (see Scott 2018), there is broad agreement about the overall negative effect and a clear indication from industry data that dulled foreign competition led to higher US metal prices.
11 Erixon et al. (2022b).
12 Ibid.
13 Heydon and Woolcock (2009).
14 The case for doing so has been amply demonstrated by recent research by Roberta Piermartini and Adam Jakubik. Their work shows that, in a scenario in which WTO members can arbitrarily increase tariffs (as they do under the unilateral application of anti-dumping penalties), countries are over four times more likely to do so than under the current regime of tariff bindings (Jakubik and Piermartini 2019).
15 For more, see Howse (2003), Coglianese and Nicolaidis (2001), and Keohane and Nye (2001).

16 Speech at the International Trade Centre's World Export Development Forum, Chongqing, China, 9 September 2010.
17 For more on this, see Nottage (2010). The economist Branco Milanović has observed that an international organization should not try to contrive equality among its members but, rather, should set itself the more realistic goal of minimizing inequity (book review of *The Meddlars* by the historian Jamie Martin, in *Foreign Affairs*, July/August 2022).
18 For more on this, see Gadbaw (2016).
19 See Rousseau (1762: 51). Rawls, for his part, makes clear that, in his examination of requirements for a well-ordered society, 'everyone is presumed to act justly and to do his part in upholding just institutions' (Rawls 1971).

Chapter 4 Battling for the Greater Good

1 In another line of research, gene sequencing of the chickpea at Murdoch University in Australia has identified 1,582 previously unknown genes, including ones that encode responses to environmental factors such as acidity, cold and oxidative stress.
2 See, for example, Saito (2023).
3 Principal sources: Global Carbon Project (www.globalcarbonproject.org) and Le Quéré et al. (2019).
4 For more on the Environmental Kuznets Curve, see Van Alstine and Neumayer (2010).
5 An earlier version of material in this section was published in August 2021 in the *East Asia Forum Weekly Digest* of the Crawford School of Public Policy at the Australian National University and subsequently republished in the *Australian Financial Review* (Heydon 2021).
6 'Two cheers for carbon tariffs', *New York Times*, 16 July 2021.
7 In China, for example, the EU Chamber of Commerce has observed that it is extremely difficult to guarantee that a firm's energy use is free from coal because of the opacity of the electricity grid (*The Economist* 'Schumpeter' column, 9 October 2021).
8 A counter from the EU could be that, on the contrary, the preferential trade agreements provide a basis for active green measures. The EU–Japan agreement, for example, contains commitments the EU could invoke to promote a more aggressive approach to trade and the environment, including that parties shall cooperate to promote the contribution of trade to the transition to low greenhouse emissions (Article 16.4).

9 *The Economist*, 28 May, 2 July 2022.
10 See Hanson and Slaughter (2023).
11 *Behind the Smokescreen: Vested Interests of EU Scientists Lobbying for GMO Deregulation*, written by Claire Robinson of GMWatch.
12 Nouveau OGM: des experts en conflit d'intérêts, *Le Monde*, 2–3 October 2022.
13 Robert Sanders, In 10 Years CRISPR transformed medicine: can it now help us deal with climate change?, *UC Berkeley Newsletter*, 30 June 2022.
14 Dennis Normile, Gene-edited foods are safe, Japanese panel concludes, *Science*, 19 March 2019.
15 COVID-19-related trade policy interventions in fact entail both trade-restricting (mainly exports) and trade-facilitating (mainly imports) measures, with the latter actually covering more trade (WTO 2021a), and with some large economies (for example, Brazil, China, India, South Africa and the United States) engaged in both restriction and facilitation (Evenett et al. 2022). However, most developing countries are likely to be those most disadvantaged by advanced-country export restrictions and least able to able to engage in import facilitation.
16 International Trade Centre Market Access Map, https://intracen.org/resources/tools/market-access-map.
17 WTO Committee on Market Access, G/MA/W/168/Rev.2, 29 March 2022.
18 See also Pauwelyn (2020).
19 Beijing was at risk of repeating that mistake with treatment drugs such as Dexamethasone and Paxlovid, which were readily available from overseas in the absence of a Chinese import ban.
20 *The Economist*, 15 October 2022.
21 Fossil fuel subsidy reduction could serve as a spur to reform, in particular, in countries where support to fossil fuel consumption has increased significantly over the past decade. In Australia, for example, revenue forgone as a result of fossil fuel subsidies over the past ten years was equivalent to over 40 per cent of the energy-related tax take, a high share by OECD standards (OECD and IEA 2021).
22 For more on this, see Asmelash (2015).
23 Marhold (2017).
24 See IEA (2021) and OECD (2023). The situation is made even more critical when major producers impose export restrictions in order to promote domestic processing and 'downstreaming',

as, for example, with the production of nickel in Indonesia or lithium in Argentina.
25 In August 2022, the World Health Organization triggered its highest level of alert in declaring the Monkey Pox virus a pandemic, with urgent implications for international public health. Yet, in the face of the pandemic, there was, globally, only one firm, Bavarian Nordic, a Danish company, supplying the only two vaccines, Jynneos and Imvanex, authorized by US and EU health authorities for use against the virus. Bavarian Nordic is also working on a vaccine against RSV, a flu-like virus, at a cost of some $300 million, leading to an expected loss of up to $40 million in 2022.
26 Jan Tinbergen applied this rule to a mathematical study of macroeconomic policy (Tinbergen 1956). It is adapted here in a broader sense. A critical question, looking ahead, is whether the Tinbergen principle will work in the burgeoning area of digital trade where data are both the facilitator of trade and the source of a non-trade concern – data privacy. Under Tinbergen's principle of separating goals, is it possible to secure the goal of data privacy without impeding the goal of data access?

Chapter 5 Arms Control
1 To the extent countries become more resilient, sanctions senders will be better able to withstand the disruption associated with sanctioning, but so will targets, making sanctions even less effective, though this is unlikely to reduce resort to them.
2 Between 1999 and 2019, the number of Americans aged twenty-five to fifty-four outside the labour force grew by 25 per cent, or 4.7 million, over six times more than the number of people who received help from the TAA.
3 For more on this, see Aghion et al. (2021), OECD (2005) and Heydon (2020).
4 *The Economist*, 24 September 2022.
5 Garnaut (2019).
6 Austin and Dougherty (2021).
7 For example, blanket bans on self-preferencing or tying, as seen in the European Commission's Digital Markets Act, may limit some beneficial behaviour. The need, rather, is for codes that prevent these practices only when they damage competition.
8 Importantly, Australia's stance in multilateral trade negotiations also opened up. In contrast with the wait-and-see attitude in earlier GATT rounds, Australia was much more proactive

in the Uruguay Round: communicating a willingness to reduce overall levels of assistance to industry; submitting an illustrative framework for the liberalization of trade in services; and seeking a tightening of the use of safeguard provisions. See Snape et al. (1998: 372).
9 The logic of this was always tenuous. Why would Europe, say, reduce its farm support in return for improved access to what, for it, was a relatively minor goods market?
10 Cited in Kelly (2008).
11 The effective rate of protection measures net protection – that is, when the cost of restrictions on imported inputs for the production of a particular product are subtracted from the protection given to that product.
12 This worsening in trade happens because, under an FTA with the EU, there are still restrictive rules of origin, reduced access (or exclusion) for some services, and non-tariff barriers via differential regulation.
13 See Tocqueville ([1856] 1986: 1078), Peyrefitte ([1976] 2006: 345) and Duhamel (2016: 134–5).
14 *The Economist*, 25 March 2023.
15 Elements of this section are drawn from an essay by the author published on 11 July 2022 in the *East Asia Forum* of the Crawford School of Public Policy at the Australian National University.
16 The agreement includes a footnote encouraging developing countries with vaccine manufacturing capacity to commit to decline to avail themselves of this option. China so committed, showing that developing country status in the WTO is not incompatible with differentiation in the application of rules.
17 See Fukuyama (2022).
18 See Ding (2022).
19 See James Laurenceson, RCEP shows that open regionalism still calls the shots, *East Asia Forum*, 30 June 2022, and Gary Hufbauer, Biden's trade policy is wrapped up in domestic and Trumpian politics, *East Asia Forum*, 12 June 2022.
20 Cerdeiro and Ruane (2022).
21 This preoccupation with threat is consistent with the view of the former Australian ambassador to China Geoff Raby that China is a constrained superpower – constrained by its geography, its history and its resource endowments (Raby 2020).
22 Online tribunals, for example, already exist to provide due

process for digital disputation, such as social media suspensions. See Susskind (2022).
23 For more on this, see Rodrik and Walt (2022).
24 See Meltzer and Kelly (2019).
25 See Erixon et al. (2022a).

References

Aghion, Philippe, Céline Antonin and Simon Bunel (2021) *The Power of Creative Destruction: Economic Upheaval and the Wealth of Nations*, trans. Jodie Cohen-Tanugi. Cambridge, MA: Belknap Press.

Antràs, Pol, and Elhanan Helpman (2004) Global sourcing, *Journal of Political Economy* 112(3): 552–80.

Anwar, Dewi Fortuna (2021) What Southeast Asia wants from the Biden presidency, *East Asia Forum Weekly Digest*, 4 April.

Armstrong, Shiro (2021) *Reimagining the Japan Relationship*. Australia-Japan Research Centre, Australian National University.

ASEAN-Japan Centre (2019) *GVCs in ASEAN*.

Asmelash, Henok (2015) Energy subsidies and WTO dispute settlement: why only renewable energy subsidies are challenged, *Journal of International Economic Law* 18(2): 261–85.

Austin, John, and Colleen Dougherty (2021) *Paths to New Prosperity in Industrial Regions of the West*. Chicago: Chicago Council on Global Affairs.

Autor, David, David Dorn and Gordon Hanson (2016a) The China shock: learning from labor-market adjustment to large changes in trade, *Annual Review of Economics* 8: 205–40.

Autor, David, David Dorn, Gordon Hanson and Kaveh Majlesi (2016b) *Importing Political Polarization? The Electoral Consequences of Rising Trade Exposure*. NBER Working Paper 22637.

Bacchetta, Marc, Eddy Bekkers, Roberta Piermartini, Stela Rubinova, Victor Stoltzenburg and Ankai Xu (2021) *COVID-19 and Global Value Chains*. WTO Research and Analysis Working Paper.

Baek, Kwang-il (1988) *Korea and the United States*. Research Center for Peace and Unification of Korea.

Baldwin, Richard (2006) Globalisation: the great unbundling(s), in *Globalisation Challenges for Europe and Finland*. Economic Council of Finland.

—— (2012) *Global Supply Chains: Why They Emerged, Why They Matter and Where They are Going*. Fung Global Institute Working Paper FGI-2012-1.

—— (2022) The peak globalisation myth, part 1, CEPR, VoxEU column, 31 August 2022; https://cepr.org/voxeu/columns/peak-globalisation-myth-part-1.

Balfour, Rosa, Lizza Bomassi and Marta Martinelli (2022) *Coronavirus and the Widening Global North–South Gap*. Carnegie Europe, 25 April.

Banerjee, Abhijit, and Esther Duflo (2022) How to prevent COVID's next comeback, *Foreign Affairs*, 21 January.

Banks, Gary (2003) Gaining from trade liberalisation: reflections on Australia's experience, in Banks, *An Economy-Wide View: Speeches on Structural Reform*. Canberra: Australian Productivity Commission.

—— (2022) A 'Rattigan man': Whitlam's assault on protection, in S. Prasser and D. Clune (eds), *The Whitlam Era: A Reappraisal*. Redland Bay, Qld: Connor Court.

Bayne, Nicholas, and Stephen Woolcock (eds) (2017) *The New Economic Diplomacy: Decision-Making and Negotiation in International Economic Relations*. 4th edn, London: Routledge.

Berden, Koen, and Joseph Francois (2015) *Quantifying Non-Tariff Measures for TTIP*. CEPS Special Report no. 116.

Bergeijk, Peter van (2009) *Economic Diplomacy and the Geography of International Trade*. Cheltenham: Edward Elgar.

—— (ed.) (2021) *Research Handbook on Economic Sanctions*. Cheltenham: Edward Elgar.

Bhagwati, Jagdish (1988) *Protectionism*. Cambridge, MA: MIT Press.
—— (1999) The 'miracle' that did happen, in E. Thorbecke and H. Wan (eds), *Taiwan's Development Experience: Lessons on Roles of Government and Market*. Amsterdam: Kluwer.
Birkel, Hendrik Sebastian, and Evi Hartman (2020) Internet of Things – the future of managing supply chain risks, *Supply Chain Management* 25(5).
Blanchard, Olivier, and Jean Tirole (2021) *Les grands défis économiques*. Paris: PUF.
Bown, Chad, and Thomas Bollyky (2021) *Here's How to Get Billions of COVID-19 Vaccine Doses to the World*. Washington, DC: Peterson Institute for International Economics.
Breckenridge, Amar, Thomas Baily and Ben Shepherd (2022) *Measuring the Impact of the EU's Approach to Open Strategic Autonomy*. Report prepared for ECIPE by Frontier Economics.
Candia, Bernardo, Olivier Coibion and Yuriy Gorodnichenko (2022) *The Macroeconomic Expectations of Firms*. NBER Working Paper 30042.
Carvalho, Vasco M., Makoto Nirei, Yukiko Saito and Alireza Tahbaz-Saehi (2020) Supply chain disruptions: evidence from the great East Japan earthquake, *Quarterly Journal of Economics* 136(2).
Cerdeiro, Diego A., and Cian Ruane (2022) *China's Declining Business Dynamism*. IMF Working Paper 22.32.
Cernat, Lucian (2022) *Processing Trade and Global Supply Chains: Towards a Resilient 'GVC 2.0' Approach*. ECIPE Policy Brief 06.
Christopher, Martin, and Helen Peck (2004) Building the resilient supply chain, *International Journal of Logistics Management* 15(2): 1–14.
Coglianese, Cary, and Kalypso Nicolaidis (2001) Securing subsidiarity: the institutional design of federalism in the United States and Europe, in K. Nicolaidis and R. Howse (eds), *The Federal Vision: Legitimacy and Levels of Governance in the United States and the European Union*. Oxford: Oxford University Press.

Colantone, Italo, and Piero Stanig (2016) *Global Competition and Brexit*. Baffi Carefin Centre Research Paper Series no. 2016-44.

Crowley, Meredith A. (2011) *Cyclical Dumping and US Antidumping Protection: 1980–2001*. Chicago: Federal Reserve Bank of Chicago.

Demarais, Agathe (2022) *Backfire: How Sanctions Reshape the World against US Interests*. New York: Columbia University Press.

Ding, Zhijie (2022) What a multi-phased reform strategy of the WTO should look like, *East Asia Forum Weekly Digest*, 7 March.

Drezner, Daniel W. (1999) *The Sanctions Paradox: Economic Statecraft and International Relations*. Cambridge: Cambridge University Press.

—— (2021) The united states of sanctions: the use and abuse of economic coercion, *Foreign Affairs*, September/October.

Drezner, Daniel W., Henry Farrell and Abraham L. Newman (2021) *The Uses and Abuses of Weaponized Interdependence*. Washington, DC: Brookings Institution Press.

Drysdale, Peter, and Shiro Armstrong (2022) How Australia can find common purpose with China, *East Asia Forum Weekly Digest*, 27 June.

Duhamel, Alain (2016) *Les Pathologies politiques françaises*. Paris: Plon.

Ebell, Monique, and James Warren (2016) The long-term impact of leaving the EU, *National Institute Economic Review* 236(1): 121–38.

Eldridge, Lucy, and Susan Powers (2018) *Imported Inputs to US Production and Productivity*. US Bureau of Labor Statistics Working Paper no. 505.

Eriksson, Katherine, Katheryn Russ, Minfei Xu and Jay Shambaugh (2019) *Trade Shocks and the Shifting Landscape of US Manufacturing*. Paper presented at the West Coast Trade Workshop, University of California, San Diego, April.

Erixon, Fredrik, Oscar Guinea, Erik van der Marel and Elena Sisto (2022a) *After the DMA, the DSA and the New AI*

Regulation: Mapping the Economic Consequences of and Responses to New Digital Regulations in Europe. ECIPE Occasional Paper 03/2022.

Erixon, Fredrik, Oscar Guinea, Philipp Lamprecht, Vanika Sharma and Renata Zilli Montero (2022b) *The New Wave of Defensive Trade Policy Measures in the European Union.* ECIPE Occasional Paper 04/2022.

European Commission (2021) *Inception Impact Assessment Instrument to Deter and Counteract Coercive Action by Third Countries.*

Evenett, Simon, Bernard Hoekman, Nadia Rocha and Michele Ruta (2021) *The COVID-19 Vaccine Production Club: Will Value Chains Temper Nationalism?* World Bank Policy Research Working Paper 9565.

Evenett, Simon, Matteo Fiorini, Johannes Fritz, Bernard Hoekman, Piotr Lukaszuk, Nadia Rocha, Michele Ruta, Filippo Santi and Anirudh Shingai (2022) Trade policy responses to the COVID-19 pandemic crisis: evidence from a new data set, *World Economy* 45(2): 342–64.

Farrell, Henry, and Abraham Newman (2019) Weaponized interdependence: how global economic networks shape state coercion, *International Security* 44(1): 42–79.

Ferrantino, Michael J. (2012) Non-tariff measures, in K. Heydon and S. Woolcock (eds), *The Ashgate Research Companion to International Trade Policy.* Farnham: Ashgate.

Flaaen, Aaron, Ali Hortaçsu and Felix Tintelot (2020) The production relocation and price effects of US trade policy: the case of washing machines, *American Economic Review* 110(7): 2103–27.

Francois, Joseph, Laura Baughman and Daniel Anthony (2018) *The Estimated Impacts of Tariffs on Steel and Aluminium.* Trade Partnership Worldwide Policy Brief.

Fukuyama, Francis (2022) A country of their own, *Foreign Affairs*, May–June.

Gadbaw, R. Michael (2016) Competition policy, in C. Cimino-Isaacs and J. J. Schott (eds), *Trans-Pacific Partnership: An Assessment.* Washington, DC: Peterson Institute for International Economics.

GAO (2006) *U.S.–China Trade: Eliminating Nonmarket Economy Methodology Would Lower Antidumping Duties for Some Companies.* Washington, DC: United States Government Accountability Office.

Garnaut, Ross (2019) *Super-Power: Australia's Low-Carbon Opportunity.* Collingwood, Vic.: La Trobe University Press.

Gaulé, Patrick (2021) Patents and the availability of essential goods in crises: the case of COVID-19 vaccines, in World Trade Organization, *World Trade Report 2021*.

Góes, Carlos, and Eddy Bekkers (2022) *The Impact of Conflicts on Trade, Growth and Innovation.* WTO Staff Working Paper ERSD-2022-09.

Goh, Evelyn (2016) Does China get what it wants in East Asia? *East Asia Forum Quarterly*, July–September.

González, Javier López, Laura Munro, Julien Gourdon, Emanuele Mazzini and Andrea Andrenelli (2019) *Participation and Benefits of SMEs in GVCs in Southeast Asia.* OECD Trade Policy Paper no. 231.

Gorokhovskaia, Yana, and Isabel Linzer (2022) The long arm of authoritarianism, *Foreign Affairs*, June.

Gupta, Sourabh (2022) China–US rivalry no new Cold War, *East Asia Forum Weekly Digest*, 21 August.

Hanson, Gordon, and Matthew Slaughter (2023) How commerce can save the climate, *Foreign Affairs*, February.

Haskel, Jonathan, and Stian Westlake (2017) *Capitalism without Capital: The Rise of the Intangible Economy.* Princeton, NJ: Princeton University Press.

Hausmann, Ricardo (2014) In search of convergence, *Project Syndicate*, 20 August.

Hayek, Friedrich (1944) *The Road to Serfdom.* London: Routledge.

Helpman, Elhanan, and Paul Krugman (1985) *Market Structure and Foreign Trade: Increasing Returns, Imperfect Competition and the International Economy.* Cambridge, MA: MIT Press.

Herskovic, Bernard, Bryan Kelly, Hanno Lustig and Stijn Van Nieuwerburgh (2020) *Firm Volatility in Granular Networks.* NBER Working Paper 19466.

Heydon, Ken (2020) *The Political Economy of International Trade*. Cambridge: Polity.

—— (2021) Asia and the Pacific: a collateral EU carbon controls target, *East Asia Forum Weekly Digest*, 8 August. www.eastasiaforum.org/author/ken-heydonwww.eastasiaforum.org/author/ken-heydon

Heydon, Ken, and Samir Makary (2006) *Assessment of Trade in Education Services in Egypt in Relation to the GATS*. Cairo: Ministry of Trade and Industry.

Heydon, Ken, and Stephen Woolcock (2009) *The Rise of Bilateralism: Comparing American, European and Asian Approaches to Preferential Trade Agreements*. Tokyo: United Nations University Press.

Hoekman, Bernard (2014) *Supply Chains, Mega Regionals and Multilateralism: A Roadmap for the WTO*. London: CEPR.

—— (2022) Green shoots for multilateral trade cooperation?, *East Asia Forum Weekly Digest*, 11 July.

Hoekman, Bernard, Anirudh Shingal, Varun Eknath and Viktoriya Ereshchenko (2021) *COVID-19, Public Procurement Regimes and Trade Policy*. World Bank Policy Research Working Paper 9511.

Howse, Robert (2003) How to begin to think about the 'democratic deficit' at the WTO, in S. Griller (ed.), *International Governance and Non-Economic Concerns: New Challenges for the International Legal Order*. New York: Springer.

Hufbauer, Gary, and Euijin Jung (2020) What's new in economic sanctions?, *European Economic Review* 130(C).

Hufbauer, Gary, Jeffrey J. Schott, Kimberley Ann Elliott and Barbara Oegg (2009) *Economic Sanctions Reconsidered*. 3rd edn, Washington, DC: Peterson Institute for International Economics.

Hufbauer, Gary, Megan Hogan and Yilin Wang (2022) How free trade can fight inflation, *Foreign Affairs*, June.

IEA (2021) *The Role of Critical Minerals in Clean Energy Transitions*.

—— (2022) *Special Report on Solar PV Global Supply Chains*.

IMF (2016) *How Large are Global Energy Subsidies?* IMF Working Paper WP/15/105.
—— (2022) *Regional Economic Outlook: Asia and the Pacific*.
IMF, OECD, World Bank and WTO (2022) *Subsidies, Trade and International Cooperation*.
Irwin, Douglas A. (2002) *Free Trade Under Fire*. Princeton, NJ: Princeton University Press.
—— (2017) *Clashing over Commerce: A History of US Trade Policy*. Chicago: University of Chicago Press.
Isaac, Grant E. (2006) The interaction between levels of rulemaking in international trade and investment: the case of sanitary and phytosanitary measures, in S. Woolcock (ed.), *Trade and Investment Rulemaking: The Role of Regional and Bilateral Agreements*. Tokyo: United Nations University Press.
ISEAS-Yusof Ishak Institute (2022) *The State of Southeast Asia: 2022 Survey Report*.
ITC (2017) *Aluminium: Competitive Conditions Affecting US Industry*. United States International Trade Commission, 4703.
Jackson, John H., and Steve Charnovitz (2012) The structure and function of the World Trade Organization, in K. Heydon and S. Woolcock (eds), *The Ashgate Research Companion to International Trade Policy*. Farnham: Ashgate.
Jain, Nitish, Karan Girotra and Serguei Netessine (2016) *Recovering from Supply Interruptions: The Role of Sourcing Strategies*. INSEAD Working Paper 2016.58.
Jakubik, Adam, and Roberta Piermartini (2019) *How WTO Commitments Tame Uncertainty*. WTO Research and Analysis Working Paper.
Jentleson, Bruce W. (2022) *Sanctions: What Everyone Needs to Know*. Oxford: Oxford University Press.
Jones, Ronald, and Henryk Kierzkowski (1990) The role of services in production and international trade: a theoretical framework, in R. Jones and A. Krueger (eds), *The Political Economy of International Trade*. Oxford: Blackwell.

Jouanjean, Marie-Agnes, Julien Gourdon and Jane Korinek (2017) *GVC Participation and Economic Transformation: Lessons from Three Sectors*. OECD Trade Policy Paper no. 207.

Kelly, Paul (2008) *The End of Certainty*. Rev. edn, London: Allen & Unwin.

—— (2016) *The Alf Rattigan Lecture: Economic Reform: A Lost Cause or Merely in Eclipse?* Australian and New Zealand School of Government, Canberra, 7 December.

Keohane, Robert, and Joseph Nye (2001) The club model of multilateral cooperation and the World Trade Organization: problems of democratic legitimacy, in R. Porter (ed.), *Efficiency, Equity and Legitimacy: The Multilateral Trading System at the Millennium*. Washington, DC: Brookings Institution.

Khandelwal, Amit, and Pablo Fajgelbaum (2022) The economic impacts of the US–China trade war, *Annual Review of Economics* 14: 205–28.

Kleinman, Benny, Ernest Liu and Stephen Redding (2020) *International Friends and Enemies*. NBER Working Paper 27587.

Konrad Adenauer Stiftung (2021) *Perception of the Planned EU Carbon Border Adjustment Mechanism in Asia Pacific: An Expert Survey*.

Krugman, Paul R. (1991) Increasing returns and economic geography, *Journal of Political Economy* 99(3): 483–99.

—— (2008) *Trade and Wages Reconsidered*. Brookings Papers on Economic Activity.

Kuznets, Simon (1953) *Shares of Upper Income Groups in Income and Savings*. Cambridge, MA: NBER.

Lawrence, Robert Z. (2017) *Recent Manufacturing Employment Growth: The Exception that Proves the Rule*. NBER Working Paper 24151.

Le Quéré, Corinne, et al. (2019) Drivers of declining CO_2 emissions in 18 developed economies, *Nature Climate Change* 9: 213–17.

Little, Ian M. D. (1996) *Picking Winners: East Asian Experience*. The Social Market Foundation, Occasional Paper.

Magistretti, Giacomo, and Marco Tabellini (2022) *Economic Integration and the Transmission of Democracy*. NBER Working Paper 30055.

Marhold, Anna (2017) *Fossil Fuel Subsidies Reform in the WTO: Options for Constraining Dual Pricing in the Multilateral Trading System*. Tilburg Law and Economics Centre Discussion Paper 2017(40).

Melitz, Marc J. (2003) The impact of trade on intra-industry reallocations and aggregate industry productivity, *Econometrica* 71(6): 1695–725.

Melitz, Marc J., and Stephen Redding (2012) *Heterogeneous Firms and Trade*. NBER Working Paper 18652.

Meltzer, Joshua P., and Cameron F. Kelly (2019) *Cyber Security and Digital Trade: Getting it Right*. Washington, DC: Brookings Institution.

Messerlin, Patrick (2004) Antidumping and safeguards, in D. Bhattasali, S. Li and W. Martin (eds), *China in the WTO: Accession, Policy Reform and Poverty Reduction*. Washington, DC: World Bank.

Messerlin, Patrick, and Stephen Woolcock (2012) Commercial instruments, in K. Heydon and S. Woolcock (eds), *The Ashgate Research Companion to International Trade Policy*. Farnham: Ashgate.

Milanović, Branko (2016) *Global Inequality: A New Approach for the Age of Globalization*. Cambridge, MA: Harvard University Press.

Miller, Chris (2022) *Chip War*. New York: Simon & Schuster.

Miroudot, Sébastien (2012) Trade and investment, in K. Heydon and S. Woolcock (eds), *The Ashgate Research Companion to International Trade Policy*. Farnham: Ashgate.

—— (2020) Reshaping the policy debate on the implications of COVID-19 for global supply chains, *Journal of International Business Policy* 3: 430–42.

Miroudot, Sébastien, and Hakan Nordstrom (2020) Made in the world? Global value chains in the midst of rising protectionism, *Review of Industrial Organization* 57(2): 195–222.

Miroudot, Sébastien, and Ben Shepherd (2012) *The Paradox*

of Preferences: Regional Trade Agreements and Trade Costs in Services, MPRA paper 41090, http://ideas.repec.org/p/pra/mprapa/41090.html.

Mulder, Nicholas (2022a) The toll of economic war: how sanctions on Russia will upend the global order, *Foreign Affairs*, March.

—— (2022b) *The Economic Weapon: The Rise of Sanctions as a Tool of Modern War*. New Haven, CT: Yale University Press.

—— (2022c) The collateral damage of a long economic war, *Foreign Affairs*, September.

Nephew, Richard (2018) *The Art of Sanctions: A View from the Field*. New York: Columbia University Press.

Nordås, Hildegunn Kyvik, Sébastien Miroudot and Przemyslaw Kowalski (2006) *Dynamic Gains from Trade*. OECD Trade Policy Working Paper no. 43.

Nottage, Hunter (2010). Evaluating the criticism that WTO retaliation rules undermine the utility of WTO dispute settlement for developing countries, in C. P. Bown and J. Pauwelyn (eds), *The Law, Economics and Politics of Retaliation in WTO Dispute Settlement*. Cambridge: Cambridge University Press.

Nye, Joseph (2004) *Soft Power: The Means to Success in World Politics*. New York: Public Affairs.

OECD (2005) *Trade and Structural Adjustment: Embracing Globalisation*.

—— (2009) *Trade Fact Sheets*.

—— (2017) *Foreign Direct Investment and the Pollution Haven Hypothesis: Evidence from Listed Firms*. OECD Economics Department Working Paper 1379.

—— (2021a) *Global Value Chains: Efficiency and Risks in the context of COVID-19*, 11 February.

—— (2021b) *Fostering Economic Resilience in a World of Open and Integrated Markets: Risks, Vulnerabilities, and Areas for Policy Action*. Report prepared for the 2021 UK presidency of the G7.

—— (2022) *The Supply of Critical Raw Materials Endangered by Russia's War on Ukraine*, August.

—— (2023) *Inventory of Export Restrictions on Industrial*

Raw Materials, https://qdd.oecd.org/subject.aspx?Subject =ExportRestrictions_IndustrialRawMaterials.

OECD and IEA (2021) *Update on Recent Progress in Reform of Inefficient Fossil Fuel Subsidies that Encourage Wasteful Consumption*.

Ostry, Jonathan David, Davide Furceri, Swarnali Ahmed Hannan and Andrew Kenan Rose (2019) *Macroeconomic Consequences of Tariffs*. IMF Working Paper WP/19/9.

Panagariya, Arvind (2008) *India: The Emerging Giant*. New York: Oxford University Press.

—— (2012) Trade openness and growth: a fresh look at Taiwan, in K. Heydon and S. Woolcock (eds), *The Ashgate Research Companion to International Trade Policy*. Farnham: Ashgate.

Pangestu, Mari, and Lili Yan Ing (2022) G20 and RCEP key to powering global recovery and development, *East Asia Forum Weekly Digest*, 28 March.

Pareto, Vilfredo ([1906] 1971) *Manual of Political Economy*. New York: Augustus M. Kelley.

Pauwelyn, Joost (2020) *Export Restrictions in Times of Pandemic: Options and Limits under International Trade Agreements*. Social Science Research Network.

Peyrefitte, Alain ([1976] 2006) *Le Mal français*. Paris: Fayard.

Pickering, Thomas (2023) How to prepare for peace talks in Ukraine, *Foreign Affairs*, March.

Piketty, Thomas (2014) *Capital in the Twenty-First Century*, trans. Arthur Goldhammer. Cambridge, MA: Harvard University Press.

Pisano, Gary P., and Willy Shih (2012) *Producing Prosperity: Why America Needs a Manufacturing Renaissance*. Cambridge, MA: Harvard Business Review Press.

Productivity Commission (2016) *Developments in Anti-Dumping Arrangements*. Canberra: Productivity Commission Research Paper.

—— (2018) *Competition in the Australian Financial System*. Draft Report, January.

Puccio, Laura (2015) *Granting Market Economy Status to China: An analysis of WTO Law and Selected WTO Members' Policy*. European Parliament.

Raby, Geoff (2020) *China's Grand Strategy and Australia's Future in the New Global Order*. Melbourne: Melbourne University Press.

Rajan, Raghuram (2019) *The Third Pillar: How Markets and the State Leave the Community Behind*. New York: Penguin Press.

Ranis, Gustav (1999) The trade-growth nexus in Taiwan's development, in E. Thorbecke and H. Wan (eds), *Taiwan's Development Experience: Lessons on Roles of Government and Market*. Amsterdam: Kluwer.

Rawls, John (1971) *A Theory of Justice*. Cambridge, MA: Harvard University Press.

Ricardo, David ([1817] 1973) *Principles of Political Economy and Taxation*. London: J. M. Dent.

Rodrik, Dani (1995) Getting intervention right: how South Korea and Taiwan grew rich, *Economic Policy* 10(20): 55–107.

Rodrik, Dani, and Stephen M. Walt (2022) Limiting great power rivalry in an anarchic world, *Foreign Affairs*, September–October.

Rousseau, Jean-Jacques (1762) *Du contrat social*. Paris: Flammarion, 1983.

Rudd, Kevin (2022) Rivals within reason, *Foreign Affairs*, July.

Saito, Kohei (2023) *Marx in the Anthropocene: Towards the Idea of Degrowth Communism*. Cambridge: Cambridge University Press.

Samuelson, Paul A. (1951) *Economics: An Introductory Analysis*. 2nd edn, New York: McGraw Hill.

Sasmal, Sunayana, and Petros Mavroidis (2022) A WTO member's home is its castle, *East Asia Forum Weekly Digest*, 15 August.

Scott, Robert E. (2018) *EPI Report*, 21 March. Economic Policy Institute.

Snape, Richard H., Lisa Gropp and Tas Luttrell (1998) *Australian Trade Policy 1965–1997: A Documentary History*. London: Allen & Unwin.

Stiglitz, Joseph E., Todd Tucker and Isabel Estevez (2022) Fighting climate change through trade, *Foreign Affairs*, July.

Stolper, Wolfgang, and Paul A. Samuelson (1941) Protection and real wages, *Review of Economic Studies* 9(1): 58–73.
Susskind, Jamie (2022) *The Digital Republic*. New York: Pegasus Books.
Taglioni, Daria, and Deborah Winkler (2016) *Making Global Value Chains Work for Development*. Washington, DC: World Bank.
Tinbergen, Jan (1956) *Economic Policy: Principles and Design*. Amsterdam: North Holland.
Tocqueville, Alexis de ([1856] 1986) *L'Ancien Régime et la Révolution*. Paris: Robert Laffont.
UK Government (2018) *EU Exit: Long-Term Economic Analysis*, Cm 9742.
UNCTAD (2014) *Trade and Development Report 2014*.
—— (2016) *Key Statistics and Trends in Trade Policy 2016*.
—— (2018) *World Investment Report*.
UNESCO (2022) *World Trends in Freedom of Expression and Media Development 2021–2022*.
US–China Economic and Security Review Commission (2021) *Annual Report to Congress*.
Van Alstine, James, and Eric Neumayer (2010) The Environmental Kuznets Curve, in K. P. Gallagher (ed.), *Handbook on Trade and the Environment*. Cheltenham: Edward Elgar.
Viner, Jacob (1950) *The Customs Union Issue*. Washington, DC: Carnegie Endowment for International Peace.
Woolcock, Stephen (2012) The evolution of the international trading system, in K. Heydon and S. Woolcock (eds), *The Ashgate Research Companion to International Trade Policy*. Farnham: Ashgate.
WTO (2001) *Accession of the People's Republic of China*, WT/L/432.
—— (2017) *World Trade Report 2017*.
—— (2021a) *Report on G20 Trade Measures: Mid-May to Mid-October 2021*.
—— (2021b) *COVID-19 Vaccine Production and Tariffs on Vaccine Inputs*. Information Note, 8 October.
—— (2021c) *Trade Policy Review of China*. WTO Secretariat Report.

—— (2021d) *World Trade Report 2021*.
—— (2022) *Report on G20 Trade Measures: Mid-May to Mid-October 2022*.
WTO and IRENA (International Renewable Energy Agency) (2021) *Trading into a Bright Energy Future*.
WTO, ITC and UNCTAD (2021) *World Tariff Profiles 2021*.
Zhao, Ziyang (2009) *Prisoner of the State: The Secret Diary of Zhao Ziyang*, ed. and trans. Bao Pu, Renee Chinag and Adi Ignatius. New York: Simon & Schuster.

Index

aerospace/aviation, 16–17, 46–7, 62, 67, 93, 100
Afghanistan, 34
Africa, 44, 98, 163–4
aggression, 33, 36, 40, 50, 53–5, 75, 139–41, 161
Aghion, Philippe, 22
Agreement on Government Procurement, 154
Agreement on Safeguards, 93
Agreement on Subsidies and Countervailing Measures (ASCM), 130
Agreement on the Application of Sanitary and Phytosanitary Measures (SPS), 13
Agreement on Trade Related Aspects of Intellectual Property Rights (TRIPS), 128, 135, 151
agriculture, 8, 48, 71, 96, 98, 102, 115, 122–3, 147–8, 153; *see also* Common Agricultural Policy
aid, 53, 66, 141; *see also* military (assistance)
Aid for Trade Initiative, 96, 109, 111
Airbus, 16–17, 61
Albanese, Anthony, 82
Alphabet, 145

Alstom, 146
aluminum, 55, 62, 93–5, 97, 100–2, 117–18, 120
Anti-Coercion Instrument (ACI), 99, 103
anti-dumping, 7–11, 87–92, 107, 120–1
Anti-Dumping Agreement, 130–1
Anti-Dumping Commission (ADC), 88
anti-globalization sentiment, 21–2, 27, 63
antitrust, 110, 145–6
Apple, 61, 146, 159
Argentina, 105, 133–4, 167
artificial intelligence, 162
Asia, 19, 43, 60, 63–4, 72–3, 128, 157
Asia-Pacific region, 107, 118, 155, 158
ASML, 56
Association of Southeast Asian Nations (ASEAN), 70–3, 80, 128, 157, 164
ASEAN E-Commerce Agreement, 164
asymmetries, 46, 56, 64, 77, 108, 165
Australia, 9, 14, 44, 80–1, 88–9, 92, 107, 114, 133, 144, 147–50,

Index

Austria, 120
autocracy, 39–40, 82–3, 162, 167
automation, 60, 72
autonomy, *see* sovereignty

Bachelet, Michelle, 48
balance of payments, 10–11, 35
Banco Delta Asia, 38
banking, 15, 19, 25, 43–4, 46, 65, 105
bankruptcy, 91, 144
Banks, Gary, 29, 148
BASF, 74, 83
batteries, 67, 104, 121, 132–3
Belarus, 62
Belgium, 43, 123
Belt and Road Initiative, 55
Bhagwati, Jagdish, 20, 142
Biden, Joe, 18–19, 40, 67–8, 102, 106, 157
blackmail, 82, 160
BMW, 121
Boeing, 16–17, 144
Bolivia, 133
Bombardier, 16–17
border procedures, 79, 96, 158
Brazil, 9, 62, 135, 155, 158, 167
Brexit, 3, 22, 149
bribery, 157
Brunei, 71
Bush, George H. W., 38
Bush, George W., 156
ByteDance, 162

Cambodia, 121
Canada, 9, 61, 77, 101, 121, 132, 149
capital, 23–4, 143
capitalism, 75, 159
Carbon Border Adjustment Mechanism (CBAM), 113, 117–21
carbon capture, 121, 123
carbon tax, 114, 116–19, 121, 124
cereal, 37, 42, 44, 92, 123, 167
chemicals, 7, 67, 74, 89, 137
Chile, 107, 133, 158
China, 9, 43, 47–9, 54–6, 61–71, 74–5, 80–4, 89–98, 110–11, 124–9, 155–61
China National Petroleum Corporation, 43
Chung Il-kwon, 36
climate change/transition, 66, 82, 97, 113–17, 119, 124, 129–31, 153, 158
Closer Economic Relations (CER), 107
coal, 45–6, 120–1, 129, 172
coercion, 33, 99, 103, 160, 171
coherence, 11, 72, 81, 93, 103, 111
Colombia, 167
Common Agricultural Policy (CAP), 25–6
comparative advantage, 17–18, 20–1, 26, 29, 59, 64, 74, 81, 133
competition, 16–17, 22, 54, 69, 75, 82–3, 100, 147, 150, 162
  import, 25–6, 29, 87
  policy, 80, 100, 104, 107, 143–6, 157–8
competitiveness, 28, 52, 60, 73, 110, 114, 156
Comprehensive and Progressive Trans-Pacific Partnership (CPTPP), 107, 110, 135, 155–6
conflict expectations model, 35–6, 39–42, 48, 50–2, 140
consumers, 43, 51, 65, 67, 72, 122–3, 141, 145

cooperation, 66, 79–82, 96, 98, 124, 133, 136, 150, 154–5, 158–9
  regional, 64, 83, 96, 106–7, 131, 142, 155–8, 164
Corden, Max, 148
Cormann, Mathias, 42
countervailing measures, 7–10, 87, 120, 130
COVAX initiative, 124, 127
COVID-19 pandemic, 61, 69, 78–9, 92, 97, 124–8, 137
Crimea, 33, 50, 77
crisis
  energy, 44, 67, 120
  food, 42
  global financial, 78, 82, 143, 145
  public health, 127
CRISPR, 114–15, 121–3, 129; see also genetic engineering
currency, 20, 27–9, 37, 46, 91
customs union, 10, 12
cyber-attacks, 34, 39, 103, 158, 164
cyber security, 69, 97, 104, 158, 161–4
Czech Republic, 62

DAF, 146
Daimler, 146
data flows, 81, 97, 156, 164
data protection, 78, 135, 151–2, 156, 162, 174
debt, 55, 66, 103; see also loans
decoupling, 46, 115–16; see also supply chain (de-linkage)
democracy, 22, 39–40, 55–6, 61, 83, 108–10, 128, 167
Deng Xiaoping, 33
dependence, 37, 56, 63, 65, 71, 78, 109, 116, 131; see also supply chain
  on China, 69–70, 80, 155
  on Russia, 45–6, 61–2, 77
deregulation, 143, 145
deterrence, 50, 99, 135
Detroit, 144
developed countries, 22, 26, 63–4, 109
developing countries, 63–4, 71–3, 78, 107, 109, 115–16, 118, 126–7, 131–7, 151, 154
digitalization, 51, 72, 79, 133–4, 158, 164; see also trade (digital)
diplomacy, 33, 52–3, 55, 103, 111, 128, 140, 155, 164
discontents of trade, 17, 139, 141–2, 161
discriminatory measures, see non-discrimination
disease, 13, 114, 123, 135; see also COVID-19 pandemic
disruption, 4, 22–4, 32, 42, 51; see also supply chain (disruption)
distortion, 8, 64, 69, 73, 76, 91–2, 97, 100, 118, 129, 141–2
diversification, 80, 143–4; see also supply chain
Drezner, Daniel, 36, 167
Drysdale, Peter, 156
Dual Circulation Strategy, 72
Dubai, 43

e-commerce, 151–2, 164
economies of scale, 59, 64, 169
economy (market/non-market), 89–91, 160, 171
education, 24, 27, 53, 108, 133, 144
efficiency, 28–9, 67, 69–70, 79, 109, 123, 142
Egypt, 25

Index

electric vehicles, 67, 104, 121, 144
electricity, 34, 43, 46, 72, 113–14, 118, 121, 132–3
electronics, 55, 62, 71, 104
embargo, 33, 43, 46, 54, 56, 126
emerging economies, 6, 155
emigration, 47, 52
emission(s), 66, 114–19, 130, 132, 172
   targets, 74, 114, 121, 129, 155
   trading system, 97, 119–20
energy, 33, 37, 42, 45–7, 51, 62–3, 79, 131–2, 141, 144
   fossil fuel, 131, 144; see also subsidy (fossil fuel)
   hydroelectric, 132
   nuclear, 14, 37, 43, 62
   solar, 48–9, 65, 67, 93, 113–14, 120–1, 133
   wind, 67
energy crisis, see crisis (energy)
energy transition, 51–2, 97, 114–17, 121, 129–30, 133, 144
engineering, 132–3
enterprise
   multinational, 63, 73, 108
   small and medium-sized (SMEs), 71, 152
   state-owned (SOEs), 43, 66, 68, 97, 110–11, 153–4, 156
environment, 60, 72, 100, 108, 113–24, 129–32, 137–8, 141, 151–2, 158, 161
Ergas, Henry, 52
Ericsson, 66, 163
espionage, 77
essential products & services, 64, 79, 120, 125, 154

Estonia, 33, 62, 77
Ethiopia, 59
ethnic minority, 33, 35; see also Uyghurs
Eurasian Economic Union, 53, 158
European Commission, 26, 46, 75, 99–100, 103, 117, 119–20, 122, 145
European Free Trade Association (EFTA), 107
European Parliament, 122
European Union, 9, 33–4, 40, 43–6, 68–71, 77–8, 98–106, 117–22, 128–9, 145–6, 149
EU Chips Act, 104
EU Digital Markets Act, 164, 174
EU Digital Services Act (DSA), 164
EU Health Emergency Preparedness and Response Authority (HERA), 136
EU–US Privacy Shield, 162
export restrictions, 10, 44, 61, 65–6, 114, 124–6, 132–3, 151–2
externalities, 127, 131, 169

Facebook, 146, 167
factory, 55, 61, 69, 78, 133–4, 144
fertilizer, 45, 63, 118
financial system, 34, 45–6, 65, 78, 154; see also services (financial)
financial transfers, 132–3, 135
fines, 145–6
finished products, 6, 58, 73
Finland, 43, 62, 77
Fisheries, see subsidy (fishing)
flexibility, 9–10, 36, 51, 53, 72, 78, 87, 125, 141, 143

food, 10, 13, 33, 42, 44–5, 97, 114, 122–3, 125, 151–2, 158
Ford, 144
foreign direct investment (FDI), 20, 48, 61, 70–5, 91, 96, 121, 152, 158
Foreign Subsidy Instrument (FSI), 100, 104
Forest Pledge, 132
forests, 115, 132
fossil fuel, *see* energy (fossil fuel); subsidy (fossil fuel)
Fossil Fuel Subsidy Reform Initiative, 131
fragmentation, 58–61, 64, 73, 78, 136, 164
France, 23, 37, 40, 43, 67, 120, 122, 150
free trade agreement (FTA), 96, 149, 158
free trade zones (China), 156
freedom, 51–2, 170
free-riding, 12, 25, 113, 116, 124
friend-shoring, 14, 57, 63–4, 76–8, 84, 141
Fumio, Kishida, 43

G7, 44, 48, 53, 79
G20, 16, 87, 131, 151, 153–5, 158, 161
Gaddafi, Muammar, 53
Garnaut, Ross, 144, 148
gas, 33, 43, 45–6, 51–2, 77, 100, 132; *see also* liquefied natural gas
Gazprombank, 43
General Agreement on Tariffs and Trade (GATT), 5, 9–11, 58, 87, 92–4, 105, 109, 119, 125, 137, 140
General Agreement on Trade in Services (GATS), 10–11, 58, 108

General Motors, 144
genetic engineering, 114–15, 122–3, 129; *see also* CRISPR
geopolitical rivalry, 32, 57, 61–3, 75–6, 82–4, 155
Georgia, 158
Germany, 34, 37, 40, 48, 51–2, 61–2, 77, 120, 141
Gladstone (Australia), 144
global value chain (GVC), 57–61, 63–4, 69–74, 76, 78–9, 82–5, 141, 154; *see also* supply chain
globalism, 72, 150, 161
globalization, 15, 35, 56–8, 64, 73–4, 161, 164; *see also* anti-globalization sentiment
Google, 145–6
governance, 64, 81, 91, 128
government, 29–30, 32, 34, 67, 73, 79–80, 91–2, 108, 142, 147
Greece (ancient), 31
green technology, 68, 121, 124, 132
growth, 19–20, 60, 63–5, 67, 69, 73, 87–8, 102–3, 115–17, 140, 143

H&M, 49
Hawke, Bob, 147–8
Hayek, Friedrich, 147
Heckscher–Ohlin–Stolper–Samuelson theory, 21, 59
Hoekman, Bernard, 152
Huawei, 54–6, 65–6, 156, 162–3
Hufbauer, Gary, 32
human rights (abuses), 33, 35, 48–50, 56, 98
Hungary, 43
hydrogen, 61, 77, 104, 114, 118, 121, 144
Hyundai, 61

Index

import, 43–4, 46, 51, 59–60, 62–3, 71, 75, 101, 104, 135, 157
 ban, 44, 49, 126
 competition, *see* competition (import)
 restrictions, 80, 97, 99, 102, 120; *see also* quantitative restrictions
 substitution, 27–9, 73, 75
 surge, *see* safeguard measures
 tariff/tax on, *see* tariffs
Important Projects of Common European Interest (IPCEI), 104
independence, 50, 54, 86
India, **9**, 43, 68, 80–1, 104–5, 116, 119, 124, 131, 134–5, 157
Indonesia, 66, 71, 89, 115, 118, 133, 149, 157
Indo-Pacific Economic Framework for Prosperity (IPEF), 157–8
Industries Assistance Commission (IAC), 148
industry policy, 10, 67, 73, 133, 164, 169
inequality, 23–4, 28, 64, 115
infant formula, 67
inflation, 18–19, 44, 46
information and communications technology (ICT), 58, 73, 93, 133
infrastructure, 44, 53, 68, 74, 79, 81, 100, 134, 144
innovation, 23–4, 29, 68, 75, 80, 114, 122, 143, 147, 165
Instrument for Supporting Trade Exchanges (INSTEX), 40
insurance, 44, 143

Intel, 65
intellectual property rights (IPR), 91, 93, 97, 99, 101, 103, 108, 110, 127–8, 134–5
interdependence, 30, 52, 56, 84, 160
intermediates, 6, 15–16, 58, 73, 75, 84
International Atomic Energy Agency, 38, 41
International Energy Agency (IEA), 116, 131–2
International Finance Corporation (IFC), 134
International Monetary Fund (IMF), 47, 78, 127, 130–1
International Procurement Initiative (IPI), 99–100, 103–4
internet, 72, 103
Internet of Things, 79, 104
InvestEU, 68
Iran, 34, 36, 40–1, 45, 82, 103, 134, 166
Iraq, 34, 40
Ireland, 146
Italy, 62
Iveco, 146

Japan, **9**, 37–8, 43, 61–2, 68–71, 77, 80–1, 111, 114, 123, 129
jobs, 22, 65, 84, 102, 117, 142
Johnson, Boris, 149
Johnson & Johnson, 134
Joint Comprehensive Plan of Action (JCPOA), 40
Joint Statement Initiative (JSI), 95, 152
Just Energy Transition Partnership (JET-P), 133

Kant, Immanuel, 84
Kazakhstan, 43

Keating, Paul, 147–8
Kenya, 59
Khashoggi, Jared, 50
Kim Il Sung, 36
Kim Jong-un, 31, 38–9, 53
knowledge, 36, 59, 68–9, 110, 124, 127–8, 137
Komatsu, 61
Korea
   Democratic People's Republic of (DPRK), 33, 37–9, 82, 141, 164
   Republic of (ROK), 9, 36–9, 62–3, **71**, 78, 89, 107, 116, 121
Krugman, Paul, 17–18, 23, 58, 117
Kuznets Curve, 24, 115

labour, 21, 26, 47, 59–60, 89, 134, 137, 158
   forced, 48–9, 53, 72, 97, 156
   law, 81, 100
   market, 23, 91, 142–4
Lamy, Pascal, 109
Laos, 71
Latvia, 33
law, 39, 45, 48–9, 81, 90–1, 93, 97, 107, 121–2, 145–6, 156
least developed countries (LDCs), 10, 96, 109, 118
Level Playing Field in the EU–UK Trade and Cooperation Agreement (LPF), 100, 104–5
liberal (trading) order, 2, 4, 20, 86, 139, 141, 147, 152–3
liberalization, 9–14, 24, 87, 96, 106, 108, 129, 137–8, 142–3, 147–8, 157–8
Libya, 53
linkages (backward/forward), 59–60, 70–1, 73, 81

liquefied natural gas (LNG), 43, 46, 51, 141, 144
Liu Xiaobo, 33
loans, 37, 133, 154; *see also* debt
lobby, 102, 147–8

machinery, 7, 47, 92–3, 104
McLaren, 144
Macron, Emmanuel, 57, 121
Malaysia, 41, 71, 115, 121, 132
manufacturing, 22, 60, 67, 71–2, 78, 81, 115, 121, 134–6, 148
market access, 53, 99–100, 106, 108, 118
market opening, 19–21, 26, 142, 147
market power, 34–5, 42, 54, 63, 74, 93–4, 106, 110, 159–61
marketing, 24, 60
MasterCard, 52
Mauritius, 158
media, 34–5, 52, 147–50, 162
medicines & medical products, 49, 53, 61–2, 67, 79–80, 114, 124–6, 134–6
Mercedes, 121
mergers & acquisitions, 55, 100, 146
metals, 61–2, 89, 118, 120, 132–3
Mexico, 12–13, 60–1, 115, 121
microchips, 46–7, 56, 66, 68
military, 14, 31, 36–7, 39–40, 47, 65–6
   assistance, 34, 36, 44, 47, 50
   conflict, 50, 56, 82
minerals, 62, 65, 67, 78, 111, 132–3
mobile devices, 59, 78, 145, 159

Moderna, 128, 134
most favoured nation (MFN), 10, 12, 96, 105
motor vehicles, 6–7, 12, 62, 71, 78, 80, 93, 102, 144, 147, 171
Mulder, Nicholas, 47, 56
multilateralism, 52–3, 94, 109–10, 119, 136, 141–2, 150–1, 154–5, 157, 164
Multiparty Interim Appeal Arbitration Agreement (MPIA), 105, 109, 152
Myanmar, 35, 45, 50, 71

national capacity, 41, 55, 65–7, 79, 113, 128, 134–5, 161
national security, 61, 93–4, 97, 99, 101, 125, 140, 161
national treatment (NT), 10, 105, 119
nationalism, 33, 94, 136
natural disaster, 84, 123
natural resources, 71, 130–1
Nayara Energy, 43
Netherlands, 56, 59, 62, 66, 120, 135
neutrality, 53, 141
New Economic Geography theory, 58
New Trade Theory, 14, 18
New Zealand, 14, 107, 122, 149
Nicaragua, 33
Nigeria, 62, 127
Nikon Corporation, 56
Nixon doctrine, 36
Nokia, 66, 163
non-discrimination, 5, 10–11, 93, 97, 99, 103, 105, 111, 118–19, 137
non-state actors, 30, 109
non-tariff measures (NTM), 6–8, 113, 120

Nord Stream, 45, 103
Nordhaus, William, 116
North American Digital Trade Zone, 164
North American Free Trade Agreement (NAFTA), 12, 60
Norway, 33

Obama, Barack, 34, 156
oil, 33, 38, 40–1, 43–6, 54, 65, 100, 116, 132
Okonjo-Iweala, Ngozi, 136, 150
Olympics, 48
Oman, 41
O'Neill, Jim, 74
Organisation for Economic Co-operation and Development (OECD), 22, 42, 69, 72, 79, 131, 154
overcapacity, 68, 97, 102
Oxford–AstraZeneca, 134

Pakistan, 82
Pangestu, Mari, 158
Papua New Guinea, 127
Paris Agreement, 119, 132
Park Chung Hee, 36
patents, 110, 128, 134–5, 151
Peru, 167
Pfizer, 58, 126, 128, 134, 136
Piketty, Thomas, 23, 116
Poland, 62, 100
policy (domestic), 71, 78–82, 84, 106, 143, 159, 164
change, 30–1, 34, 50, 83, 124, 146
makers/making, 50–1, 63, 76, 94, 106, 129, 139–41
political parties, 21, 41, 65, 146–7, 150
Poonawalla, Adar, 126
population ageing, 72, 139, 159

populism, 161
ports, 14, 38, 62, 144, 158
Portugal, 46
precautionary measures, *see* scientific evidence
preferential trade agreement (PTA), 11–14, 58, 64, 107, 120, 135, 137, 149, 156–9
prices, 21, 43–6, 59, 62, 67, 74, 87–90, 92, 102, 131
product design, 24, 60, 72, 144
productivity, 28–9, 69, 81, 147, 159, 161, 164
proportionality, 11, 93, 103, 111
protection of human, animal or plant life or health, 10, 119, 124–5, 137, 140, 153
protectionism, 58, 87–9, 92, 94, 103, 113, 116, 118–21, 124, 142, 148
protectionist capture, 24–6, 51, 76, 102, 106, 116–17, 124, 153, 161
public health, 108, 113–14, 121–2, 125–9, 133, 137–41, 161
public investment, 79, 124, 137
public opinion, 21, 32, 34–5, 39, 124, 140, 142, 145, 149–50
public procurement, 7, 66–7, 99–100, 103–4
Pulsic, 55
Putin, Vladimir, 31, 42, 44, 47, 50–1, 140

quantitative restrictions (QRs), 7, 9–10, 20, 92, 102, 117, 147

raw materials, 6, 61, 63, 77, 125
recession, 22, 37, 46–7, 69, 94

regime change, 33
Regional Comprehensive Economic Partnership (RCEP), 83, 107, 156–8
regionalization, 76, 78; *see also* cooperation (regional)
regulatory
    barriers, 13, 26–7, 121
    framework, 27, 45, 72, 81, 134, 143–7
    sovereignty, 27, 108
rehabilitation, 50
Renault, 146
RepowerEU, 68
research/R&D, 24, 67, 121–3, 135, 144
re-shoring, 57, 61, 64, 66–7, 69, 73–6, 78, 84, 141
resilience, 51, 63, 141, 157–9; *see also* supply chain
resistance, 26, 147, 150, 160, 167
resource allocation, 29, 75, 91, 165
retaliation, 45, 51, 66, 102–5, 120, 153, 161
retribution, 34, 50
returns to scale, 18, 73
Ricardo, David, 17–18, 21, 59, 74
Rodrik, Dani, 19, 23
Rolls Royce, 144
Romania, 100
Roosevelt, Franklin, 54
Rosneft, 43
Rousseau, Jean-Jacques, 111
Rudd, Kevin, 75
rules-based trading order, 86–7, 98, 103, 108–9, 112, 129, 140–1, 151, 154, 156
    breach of, 85–6, 93, 98, 119
rules of origin (ROO), 8, 11–12, 157

Index

Russia, 33–5, 37–9, 41–53, 61–2, 82, 94, 104–5, 128–9, 131, 166
Rwanda, 134

safeguard measures (import surge), 10, 16, 87, 92–3
Samsung, 66, 78
sanctions, 31–54, 56, 98, 103, 140–1, 161, 164
   financial, 31–2, 34, 46, 53, 65
   military, 32
   relief, 38–9, 52–3, 141
   vulnerability, 37, 46, 56
sanitary and phytosanitary measures (SPS), 7, 13, 97, 108–9
Sanofi, 134
Sarawak Energy, 132
Saudi Arabia, 40, 50, 131
Scandinavia, 66, 143
Scholz, Olaf, 61
scientific evidence, 13, 97, 109, 122, 137
Sechin, Igor, 43
self-harm, 27–9, 31, 51, 65, 67, 81, 102
self-reliance, 56–7, 64, 68, 74, 84–6, 152–4, 160–1
semiconductors, 46, 54–6, 65–9, 100, 104
Senegal, 62, 134
sensitive products and services, 6, 12, 64, 74–5, 89, 108, 162
services, 64, 78, 115; *see also* trade (in services)
   financial, 11, 27, 32, 91, 96, 143
   public, 111, 156
Sheffield, 144
Shevardnadze, Eduard, 37
shipping, 38, 42, 44–5, 62
Shoigu, Sergei, 42
Siemens, 146
silicon, 49, 65, 113, 120
Singapore, 71, 107, 132, 134, 158
Sinopharm/Sinovac, 128
SK Hynix, 66
skill, 21, 24, 26, 29, 47, 59
Slovakia, 43
Smoot–Hawley tariffs, 94
social security, 143
socialism, 75, 161
Somalia, 34
South Africa, 134, 155
sovereignty, 72, 86, 93–5, 98–9, 106, 109–11, 141, 149, 152–3, 161; *see also* regulatory (sovereignty)
Soviet Union, 37, 75, 159, 161
Spain, 46, 58
specialization, 20, 58–9, 64
Sri Lanka, 62
steel, 62, 89, 93–5, 100–2, 106, 114, 116–20
Stellantis, 121, 144
Stiglitz, Joseph, 117
stock management, 51, 77, 79
structural adjustment, 22–3, 142–3, 160
subsidy, 7–8, 67–9, 75–6, 95–8, 100, 104, 110, 117–18, 135–6, 153–6, 161
   export, 10, 87
   customer, 46, 121
   fishing, 97–8, 129, 143, 151
   fossil fuel, 120, 124, 130–1, 141, 151, 155
supply chain, 48–9, 73, 119, 136, 153, 158
   de-linkage, 64, 66, 69–70, 72, 75–6, 80–1, 133
   dependence, 57, 62, 64, 67, 69, 113

supply chain (*cont.*)
  disruption, 32, 57, 60–1, 69, 72, 76–7, 125–6, 164
  diversification, 63, 68, 76–8
  resilience, 72, 76–81, 84–5, 158, 164
  shock, 60–1, 63, 69, 72, 76, 78–9, 84, 154
  vulnerability, 60, 63, 69, 72, 75–7, 79, 154, 161
  see also global value chain
Supply Chain Resilience Initiative (SCRI), 80–1
sustainability, 64, 114, 117, 130, 152
SWIFT, 15, 43, 46
Syria, 45

Taiwan, 19–20, 50, 54–6, 58
Taiwan Semiconductor Manufacturing Company (TSMC), 55, 66, 69
tariffs, 5–10, 16, 27–8, 61, 73, 92–6, 101–2, 116–17, 120–1, 134, 147
taxation, 24, 46, 57, 146, 168; *see also* carbon tax
technical barriers to trade (TBT), 8, 162
technology, 56, 63, 65–6, 75, 78, 80–1, 92, 114–16, 120–1, 162–3
telecoms, 25, 47, 54, 66, 145, 162–3, 171
territorial integrity, 33, 39, 50, 53, 80, 141
terrorism, 53, 84, 160
textiles, 6, 48–9, 59, 67, 72, 98, 147
Thailand, 61, 66, 71, 84, 121, 159
threat, 16–17, 32, 36–7, 54–6, 87, 93, 110, 116, 124, 150
3M, 79

Tiananmen massacre, 34, 161
TikTok, 162
Tinbergen, Jan, 137–8
Tirole, Jean, 116
Toll Holdings, 45
Toshiba, 61
Toyota, 121
trade
  costs, 12, 58, 118
  creation and diversion, 14, 157
  gains from, 14, 17–18, 25, 29, 57–9, 83, 124, 140, 142–3, 150
  injury, 10, 87–8, 130
  remedy, 7, 86–7, 89, 92–3, 98–9, 101–3, 106–7, 110, 141, 152–3, 161
  weapon, 1–4, 32, 49, 64, 83–4, 92–4, 101–2, 120, 124, 136–41, 149
trade (types of)
  digital, 74, 81, 133, 156–7, 161–4
  in goods, 14, 26, 75
  intra-industry, 14–15, 18, 26, 58
  in services, 14–15, 32, 58, 74, 99, 101, 105–6, 131–3, 152, 164; *see also* General Agreement on Trade in Services
  in value added (TiVA), 59–60, 71
Trade and Health Initiative (TAHI), 136
Trade and Technology Council (TTC), 162
Trade Policy Review, 95–8, 109
trade union, 117, 122
transparency, 96–7, 100, 109, 123, 125–6, 131, 143, 163
transport, 46, 53, 61–2, 79
travel ban, 33, 46, 50

Index

Treaty on the Non-Proliferation of Nuclear Weapons, 38
Trebeck, David, 148
Trump, Donald, 28–9, 34, 38, 40–1, 54–5, 61, 93–5, 101–2, 106
trust, 52, 63, 112, 128–9, 142, 149–50, 162, 164
Türkiye, 62, 100

Ukraine, 33, 41–4, 53, 62, 120, 141; see also war (in Ukraine)
unemployment, 22, 28, 142–3
unilateralism, 35, 54–5, 85–6, 93–4, 96, 98–9, 101, 104–7, 141, 153
unintended consequences, 40–1, 66, 133, 162
United Arab Emirates, 41
United Kingdom, 44, 54–6, 62, 100, 102, 104–5, 144, 149, 158, 163
United Nations (UN), 33–4, 38–9, 53, 83
  UN Conference on Trade and Development (UNCTAD), 61, 78, 154
  UN World Food Programme, 151
United States, 9, 33–4, 36–8, 44–6, 65–8, 80–1, 92–5, 101–2, 120–1, 126, 144–6
US CHIPS and Science Act, 68
US Congress, 5, 139, 157
US Defense Production Act, 67, 126
US Department of Commerce, 16, 48, 65–6
US Department of Justice, 146
US Department of the Treasury, 28, 48, 63, 65, 74

US Federal Reserve Board, 19, 92
US Inflation Reduction Act, 68, 121
US Infrastructure Act, 68
US International Trade Commission (ITC), 17, 92, 102
US Trade Act, 93
US Trade Adjustment Assistance (TAA), 143
US Trade Expansion Act, 93
US–China Economic and Security Review Commission, 91–2
United States–Mexico–Canada Agreement (USMCA), 12–13, 132, 171
Updated Enforcement Regulation for Trade Disputes (ER), 100–1, 105–6
Uyghur Forced Labour Prevention Act, 49
Uyghurs, 35, 47–9, 53, 55, 72, 98, 160

vaccines, 53, 58, 96, 110, 114, 124–8, 134–5, 151
Valeo, 59
values, 3, 12, 34, 109, 128
Venezuela, 44,
Vietnam, 66, 71, 78, 121, 157, 159
virtual private network (VPN), 52, 167
Visa, 52
vulnerability, 118, 127; see also sanctions (vulnerability); supply chain (vulnerability)

wages, 13, 59–60, 91, 102
Wagner Group, 31, 39
Walsh, Maximilian, 148

WannaCry ransomware, 164
war, 23–4, 34–5, 84
  Cold, 37, 39, 75
  Second World, 35, 54
  in Ukraine, 35, 39, 41–5, 47, 50, 52–3, 61–2, 120, 140, 166–7
water, 100
weapons, 33, 38–40, 53
  nuclear, 31–3, 36–41, 50, 141
welfare, 14, 149
WhatsApp, 146
Whirlpool, 92
Whitlam, Gough, 147–8
Wilhelmshaven, 51, 141
Wilson, Woodrow, 34
Wingtech, 55
winners and losers, 21–4, 67, 73, 81, 142, 162
Woolcock, Stephen, 9
workers, 21, 74, 121, 137, 143–4, 154
World Bank, 53, 69, 117, 154
World Health Organization (WHO), 127, 174

World Trade Organization (WTO), 68, 83–99, 105, 107–11, 124–6, 129–31, 135–7, 150–55
WTO Appellate Body, 94–5, 101, 105, 110, 125, 152–3
WTO disciplines, 68, 83, 93, 95, 130–1, 151
WTO dispute settlement, 86, 92–5, 105, 107, 109–11, 130, 135, 137, 151–3, 155
WTO Ministerial Conference (MC12), 110, 128–9, 131, 150–3, 155
WTO Technical Barriers to Trade Committee, 162

Xi Jinping, 33, 48, 57, 82, 159–60
Xinjiang, 48–50, 53, 55, 156

Yellen, Janet, 63

Zhao Ziyang, 160–1
Zheng Zeguang, 55
ZTE, 66